The Ultimate Beginners Guide to Fix and Flip Real Estate Investing

Real Estate Investing, Volume 8

Jim Pellerin

Published by Jim Pellerin, 2023.

THE ULTIMATE BEGINNERS GUIDE TO FIX AND FLIP REAL ESTATE INVESTING

First edition. May 7, 2023.

ISBN: 979-8223705499

Written by Jim Pellerin.

Also by Jim Pellerin

Real Estate Investing

Real Estate Investing Strategies: The Secret to Financial Independence with Real Estate
Real Estate Investing with Lease Options - Investing in Real Estate with No Money Down
Invest Now - The Passive Approach to Winning at Real Estate
The Ultimate Beginners Guide to Real Estate Investing
The 98 Best Real Estate Investing Strategies
The Ultimate Beginners Guide to Wholesale Real Estate Investing
The Ultimate Beginners Guide to Rental Real Estate Investing
The Ultimate Beginners Guide to Fix and Flip Real Estate Investing

Watch for more at www.jimpellerin.com.

Table of Contents

The Ultimate Beginners Guide to Fix and Flip Real Estate Investing

An Overiew of Fix and Flip

Real Estate Investing

Jim Pellerin

Updated for 2023

Why You Should Read This Book

Most people who want to get started with Real Estate Investing, have no idea how to get sarted. Or worse, they have some idea how to get started but it is the wrong strategy for them.

This book provides an overview of how to get started in Fix and Flip Real Estate Investing. This book is NOT a practical approach to Fix nd Flip Real Estate Investing and the reader is NOT expected to be able to start investing in fix and flips after completing this book.

In this book, you will learn enough information to be able to decide if fix and flip real estate investing is right for you.

The Ultimate Beginners Guide to Fix and Flip Real Estate Investing

Chapter 1: Introduction to Fix and Flip Real Estate Investing

Flip - Photo by Taylor Hunt

Real estate investing is a popular investment strategy that offers great potential for **generating wealth**. One particular method of real estate investing that has gained popularity in recent years is fix and flip real estate investing.

Fix and flip real estate investing involves purchasing a property, making improvements to it, and then selling it for a profit.

In this chapter, we will provide an overview of fix and flip real estate investing, including why it is a great investment strategy, how to get started, the benefits and risks involved, understanding the real estate market, and key skills and characteristics of successful fix and flip investors.

1.1 Why Fix and Flip Real Estate Investing is a Great Investment Strategy

Fix and flip real estate investing can be a great investment strategy for several reasons.

1. Firstly, it allows investors to generate income in a relatively **short period of time**. Unlike other forms of real estate investing, such as rental properties, fix and flip investments can often be completed within a *matter of months.*
2. Secondly, fix and flip investing provides investors with the opportunity to use their skills and knowledge to **add value** to a property. By renovating a property, investors can increase its value and *sell it for a higher price* than what they originally paid for it.
3. Finally, fix and flip investing can offer investors a **high return on investment (ROI)**. If done correctly, investors can make a *significant profit* on a single investment, making it a highly attractive investment option.

1.2 How to Get Started in Fix and Flip Real Estate Investing

Getting started in fix and flip real estate investing requires a few key steps.

1. Firstly, investors should research the market and **identify potential properties** that are *undervalued* or have the *potential for improvements*. It is important to have a good understanding of the local real estate market and the potential resale value of the property after improvements have been made.
2. Secondly, investors will need to **secure financing** for the investment. This may involve obtaining a *mortgage* or a *loan*

from a financial institution. Investors will need to have a good credit score and demonstrate financial stability to obtain financing.

3. Thirdly, investors will need to create a **budget and plan for the renovations**. This will involve *estimating the cost of the renovations*, as well as any other associated costs such as *property taxes*, *insurance*, and *utility bills*.
4. Finally, investors will need to **hire contractors** and other professionals to carry out the renovations. It is important to ensure that all work is carried out to a high standard and that the *renovations are completed* on time and within budget.

1.3 The Benefits and Risks of Fix and Flip Real Estate Investing

While fix and flip real estate investing can offer investors significant rewards, there are also risks involved.

1. One of the primary risks is the potential for **unexpected costs** to arise during the renovation process. This could include *structural issues*, *zoning or permit issues*, or unexpected *changes in the market*.
2. Another risk is that the property **may not sell for the expected price**, resulting in a *smaller profit* or even a *loss*. Finally, fix and flip investors may face *competition from other investors*, which could drive up the purchase price of properties and reduce profit margins.

However, despite these risks, fix and flip real estate investing can offer investors significant benefits. These include:

1. the potential for **high return on investment,**
2. the ability to use skills and knowledge to **add value to a**

property, and
3. the opportunity to generate income in a relatively **short period of time**.

1.4 Understanding the Real Estate Market for Fix and Flip Investing

Understanding the real estate market is crucial for successful fix and flip investing.

1. Investors will need to **research local market trends** and the **potential demand** for renovated properties in the area.
2. It is also important to consider the **location of the property**, as this can have a significant impact on its resale value.
3. In addition, investors should have a good understanding of the **costs involved in the renovation process**, including *materials*, *labor*, and other expenses such as *permits*, *taxes*, and *insurance*.

By understanding the real estate market and associated costs, investors can make informed decisions about which properties to invest in and how much to budget for renovations.

1.5 Key Skills and Characteristics of Successful Fix and Flip Investors

Successful fix and flip investors possess a range of key skills and characteristics.

1. Firstly, they have a good **understanding of the real estate market** and are able to identify undervalued properties with potential for improvement.
2. Secondly, successful fix and flip investors are skilled in **project management** and have the ability to create a *realistic*

budget and timeline for the renovation process. They are also able to *oversee contractors* and ensure that the work is carried out to a high standard.

3. Thirdly, successful fix and flip investors have **strong financial management skills** and are able to *secure financing* and *manage the associated costs* of the investment.
4. Finally, successful fix and flip investors have a **strong work ethic** and are able to *manage the stress and uncertainty* associated with real estate investing.

Conclusion

Fix and flip real estate investing can be a highly attractive investment strategy for those looking to **generate income in a relatively short period of time**. However, it is important to understand the risks involved and to possess the key skills and characteristics necessary for success.

By understanding the real estate market, creating a realistic budget and timeline, and hiring the right professionals, investors can minimize risk and maximize returns on their fix and flip investments. With the right strategy and approach, fix and flip real estate investing can be a highly profitable investment option.

Chapter 2: Flipping Houses vs. Holding Properties: Pros and Cons

Portfolio - uncredited

Real estate investing offers a variety of investment strategies to choose from. Two popular approaches are **flipping houses** for short-term profits and **holding properties** for long-term cash flow. In this chapter, we will discuss the pros and cons of each strategy, as well as how to determine which approach is best for your investment goals.

2.1 Understanding the Differences Between Flipping and Holding Properties

Flipping a property involves:

1. purchasing a distressed property at a low price,
2. renovating it, and
3. then selling it quickly for a profit.

Holding a property, on the other hand, involves:

1. purchasing a cash-flowing property,
2. renting it out for passive income, and
3. allowing it to appreciate over the long term.

Key differences:

1. One of the key differences between flipping and holding properties is the **time horizon** for the investment. Flipping a property typically requires a *much shorter timeline*, typically ranging from a few months to a year. In contrast, holding a property is a *long-term investment* that may span several years or even decades.
2. Another key difference is the **level of involvement** required. Flipping a property requires a *significant amount of work*, including finding and purchasing a property, overseeing renovations, and finding a buyer. Holding a property requires *ongoing management*, including finding tenants, handling maintenance requests, and collecting rent.

2.2 Pros and Cons of Flipping Houses for Short-Term Profits

Flipping houses can be an attractive strategy for investors seeking high returns in a relatively short period of time.

Pros

- One of the biggest advantages of flipping is the potential for **significant profits**. By purchasing a distressed property and renovating it, investors can increase the value of the property and sell it for a profit.

- Flipping also allows investors to quickly move on to the next investment opportunity, providing the potential for multiple profitable deals in a relatively **short period of time**.

Cons

- Flipping houses comes with a number of risks and challenges. One of the biggest risks is **unexpected renovation costs**. Renovations can be difficult to estimate, and unexpected issues can arise during the renovation process, leading to higher costs than anticipated.
- Additionally, it can be **difficult to find a buyer** in a slow market, which can delay the sale and reduce profits. Flipping also comes with potential tax implications, including short-term capital gains taxes.

2.3 Pros and Cons of Holding Properties for Long-Term Cash Flow

Holding properties can provide investors with steady rental income and long-term appreciation.

Pros

- One of the biggest advantages of holding properties is the potential for **passive income**. By renting out a property, investors can generate *cash flow* that can help cover mortgage payments and other expenses.
- Holding properties can also provide **long-term appreciation and increased wealth** as property values increase over time.

Cons

- However, holding properties requires a **longer-term commitment** and involves *ongoing maintenance* and *management responsibilities.* Investors must be prepared to handle tenant turnover, maintenance requests, and other issues that may arise.
- Additionally, **rental income can be impacted** by *market fluctuations* and the expenses associated with *vacancy* and *tenant turnover.*

2.4 How to Decide Which Strategy is Right for Your Investment Goals

When considering which strategy is right for your investment goals, it is important to consider factors such as your *desired level of involvement*, the *timeline for return on investment*, and overall investment objectives.

- For investors seeking **short-term gains,** *flipping houses* may be more appropriate. Flipping provides the potential for significant profits in a relatively short period of time. However, investors must be prepared to take on the risks and challenges associated with flipping, including *unexpected renovation costs* and the potential for a *slow market.*
- For investors seeking **long-term cash flow** and **appreciation**, *holding properties* may be a better fit. Holding properties provides the potential for *passive income* and *long-term appreciation*. However, investors must be prepared for the *ongoing management* responsibilities and potential *market fluctuations*.

2.5 Strategies for Balancing Your Fix and Flip and Rental Property Investments

For those who wish to pursue both fix and flip and rental property investments, there are strategies to balance these two approaches.

1. One strategy is to **use the profits** from flipping properties to *fund the purchase of rental properties*. This can help investors build a portfolio of rental properties over time while still taking advantage of the short-term gains from flipping.
2. Another strategy is to focus on flipping properties in areas where *rental demand is high*. By flipping properties in areas with high rental demand, investors can potentially sell the property quickly and still **have the option to hold onto it** and generate rental income.

Ultimately, the key to successfully balancing fix and flip and rental property investments is to have a *clear investment strategy* and to stay disciplined in executing that strategy. Investors should carefully consider their investment goals and risk tolerance, and develop a plan that aligns with those goals.

Conclusion

Flipping houses and holding properties are two popular real estate investment strategies, each with its own set of pros and cons. While flipping can provide investors with short-term gains, holding properties can provide long-term cash flow and appreciation. When deciding which strategy to pursue, investors should consider:

1. their desired level of involvement,
2. the timeline for return on investment, and
3. overall investment objectives.

Additionally, there are strategies to **balance these two approaches**, including using profits from flipping to fund rental property purchases and focusing on flipping properties in areas with high rental demand. By carefully considering their options and staying disciplined in executing their investment strategy, investors can successfully navigate the world of fix and flip and rental property investments.

Chapter 3: Analyzing Real Estate Market Trends

Market trends - Photo by Carlos Muza

Real estate investing can be a lucrative way to build wealth, but success requires a thorough *understanding of the real estate market cycle and trends*. In this chapter, we will explore the key concepts and strategies for analyzing real estate market trends and making informed investment decisions.

3.1 Understanding the Real Estate Market Cycle and Trends

The real estate market cycle refers to the natural pattern of ups and downs in the housing market. It is composed of four stages: expansion, peak, contraction, and trough.

1. During the **expansion stage**, housing *prices are rising, demand is high*, and *inventory is low.*
2. The **peak stage** is marked by a *slowdown in price growth* and a

shift towards a more *balanced market.*

3. In the **contraction stage**, *prices begin to decline*, and *demand decreases.*
4. The **trough stage** is characterized by *low prices, high inventory*, and *low demand.*

Understanding the current stage of the real estate market cycle is essential for making informed investment decisions. For example, during the expansion stage, investors may focus on acquiring properties with high appreciation potential, while during the trough stage, they may look for undervalued properties with potential for growth.

To determine the current stage of the real estate market cycle, investors can look at a variety of indicators, including *housing prices, inventory levels*, and the overall *state of the economy*. In addition, investors should stay up-to-date on *market trends* and monitor local and national data sources.

3.2 Analyzing Local and National Market Indicators for Fix and Flip Investing

To make informed investment decisions, real estate investors must analyze both local and national market indicators.

Local indicators include factors such as:

1. population growth,
2. job growth, and
3. median income levels.

National indicators include factors such as:

1. interest rates,
2. inflation, and

3. the overall state of the economy.

For fix and flip investors, **local market indicators** are particularly important, as they can help identify neighborhoods with *high demand for renovated properties*. Investors should look for areas with a high demand for housing, low inventory, and a growing population.

In addition, investors should consider factors such as the *condition of the property*, the *cost of renovations*, and the *potential resale value*. By carefully analyzing these factors and staying up-to-date on market trends, fix and flip investors can make informed decisions and maximize their profits.

3.3 Predicting Future Market Trends for Better Investing Decisions

While no one can predict the future of the real estate market with certainty, investors can use data and historical trends to make informed predictions about future market trends. By analyzing factors such as *population growth*, *job growth*, and *housing inventory*, investors can make informed decisions about where to invest and when to invest.

It's important to note that predicting future market trends is not an exact science, and there is always a degree of uncertainty. However, by **staying informed about market trends** and regularly **analyzing data**, investors can make better-informed decisions and reduce their risk of loss.

In addition, investors should be prepared to **adjust their strategies** as market conditions change. This may involve shifting focus to *different types of properties* or *investing in new markets*. By staying flexible and adaptable, investors can maximize their returns and mitigate risks.

3.4 Understanding the Impact of Economic and Political

Factors on Real Estate Markets

Economic and political factors can have a significant impact on the real estate market. For example, **changes in interest rates** can affect the affordability of mortgages and impact demand for housing. Similarly, **changes in government policies**, such as *tax incentives* or *zoning regulations*, can influence the supply and demand of housing.

To make informed investment decisions, investors should:

1. stay informed about **economic and political factors** that may impact the real estate market. This may involve *monitoring government policies*, *economic indicators*, and *news sources*.
2. In addition, investors should be prepared to **adjust their strategies** as market conditions change.
3. Finally, investors should be aware of the **potential risks** associated with economic and political instability. For example, a *recession* or *political crisis* can lead to a decline in housing prices and lower demand for properties.

Investors should be prepared to weather these types of events by maintaining a **diversified portfolio** and having a solid financial plan in place.

3.5 Strategies for Investing in a Changing Market

Investing in a changing market requires a flexible and adaptable approach.

1. One strategy is to **diversify your portfolio** by investing in a variety of *property types* and *locations*. This can help mitigate risk and ensure that you have exposure to different market segments.

2. Another strategy is to **focus on long-term growth** rather than short-term gains. By identifying areas with strong potential for growth and investing in high-quality properties, investors can position themselves for long-term success.
3. Finally, investors should be prepared to **adjust their strategies** as market conditions change. This may involve shifting focus to *different types of properties* or *investing in new markets*. By staying flexible and adaptable, investors can maximize their returns and mitigate risks.

Conclusion

Analyzing real estate market trends is essential for making informed investment decisions. By understanding the real estate market cycle, analyzing local and national market indicators, predicting future market trends, understanding the impact of economic and political factors, and developing flexible investment strategies, investors can position themselves for long-term success. While no one can predict the future of the real estate market with certainty, by staying informed and adaptable, investors can mitigate risks and maximize their returns.

Chapter 4: Building a Network for Fix and Flip Investing

Networking - Photo by Product School

Real estate investing can be a lucrative venture, but it requires a lot of effort, time, and resources. To be successful, fix and flip investors need a strong network of professionals, industry experts, and other investors who can offer valuable insights, resources, and opportunities. In this chapter, we will explore why networking is important for real estate investing, strategies for building a strong real estate network, and how to leverage your network for greater success.

4.1 Why Networking is Important for Real Estate Investing

Networking is critical for real estate investors, especially those who are involved in fix and flip investing.

1. A strong network provides **access to essential resources** such as *lenders*, *contractors*, *real estate agents*, and other service

providers that can help investors find, purchase, and renovate properties.

2. Networking also offers opportunities to **learn from other investors and industry experts**, exchange ideas and insights, and avoid common mistakes.
3. Building a robust network is essential to **stay up-to-date on market trends** and changes, and have access to potential investment opportunities.
4. Investors can also benefit from networking by **gaining exposure to new investment opportunities** that they may not have found on their own.

This is why networking is an essential part of building a successful real estate investing business.

4.2 Strategies for Building a Strong Real Estate Network

Building a strong real estate network requires a proactive and intentional approach.

1. One strategy is to **attend local real estate investor meetings and events**, where investors can meet and connect with other investors, industry experts, and service providers.
2. **Online forums and social media groups** can also be a great way to connect with other investors and professionals in the industry.
3. Another strategy is to actively seek out and **build relationships with real estate professionals**, such as *real estate agents*, *brokers*, and *property managers*. These professionals can provide valuable insights into local market conditions and help investors identify potential investment opportunities.

It is crucial to be genuine and authentic when networking, seeking to build relationships based on trust and **mutual benefit**.

4.3 Finding and Working with Real Estate Professionals

Real estate professionals are an essential part of any successful real estate investing business. They can help investors:

1. identify potential investment opportunities,
2. connect them with other professionals, and
3. provide valuable insights into local market conditions.

Real estate agents, brokers, and property managers can help investors **find and purchase properties** and **market and sell the finished product**.

When working with real estate professionals, investors must find someone who is experienced, trustworthy, and understands their specific investing goals. They should also communicate openly and honestly with their real estate professionals to ensure that they are on the same page and working towards the same objectives.

4.4 Building Relationships with Other Investors and Industry Experts

Building relationships with **other investors** and industry experts can be highly beneficial for fix and flip investors. Attending real estate conferences and workshops, participating in online forums and mastermind groups, and seeking out mentorship opportunities are strategies for building relationships with other investors and industry experts.

When building relationships with other investors and industry experts, it is important to approach the interaction as a **mutual exchange of**

knowledge and insights. Investors should seek to learn from other experienced investors, share their own experiences, and collaborate on potential investment opportunities. This can lead to valuable **partnerships**, **joint ventures**, and increased **access to investment opportunities**.

Additionally, industry experts such as *contractors*, *architects*, and *lenders* can provide valuable insights and resources to help investors succeed in fix and flip investing.

It is important to establish relationships with these professionals to ensure that investors have access to the best resources and can avoid potential pitfalls.

4.5 How to Leverage Your Network for Greater Success in Fix and Flip Investing

To leverage their network for greater success in fix and flip investing, investors should take advantage of the resources and opportunities available to them.

1. As previously mentioned, this can include *attending networking events* and *conferences*, joining *online forums* and *social media groups*, and seeking out *mentorship opportunities*.
2. Investors should also be willing to **share their own experiences and knowledge** with others in their network. By being a valuable resource and offering support to others, investors can strengthen their relationships and create opportunities for collaboration and **joint ventures**.
3. Finally, investors should be proactive in seeking out potential investment opportunities and using their network to **find deals**. This can involve reaching out to other investors or real estate professionals in their network or collaborating with other investors on joint ventures.

Conclusion

Building a strong network is essential for fix and flip investors looking to succeed in the competitive real estate market. By actively seeking out and building relationships with other investors, industry experts, and real estate professionals, investors can gain access to valuable resources, insights, and opportunities. It is important to approach networking with authenticity, openness, and a willingness to learn and collaborate with others. With a strong network in place, investors can leverage their resources and achieve greater success in fix and flip investing.

Chapter 5: Finding Profitable Fix and Flip Properties

Properties - Photo by Breno Assis

Fix and flip properties can be a great investment opportunity for real estate investors looking to make quick profits. However, not all properties are suitable for fix and flip projects, and not all markets offer the same level of potential returns. Finding profitable fix and flip properties requires careful research, analysis, and due diligence. In this chapter, we will explore the criteria for profitable fix and flip properties, the best markets for fix and flip investing, strategies for finding and analyzing fix and flip properties, tips for evaluating property condition and rehab costs, and how to make offers and negotiate deals for fix and flip properties.

5.1 Understanding the Criteria for Profitable Fix and Flip Properties

The first step in finding profitable fix and flip properties is to understand the criteria that make a property suitable for this type of investment.

1. One of the most important factors to consider is the **property's location**. Properties in desirable neighborhoods with high demand and limited supply are more likely to attract buyers and generate higher profits.
2. Other factors to consider include the property's **size, layout, and condition**. Properties that require cosmetic upgrades or minor repairs are often the best candidates for fix and flip projects, as they offer the potential for quick and easy returns on investment.
3. Another important factor to consider is the **purchase price** of the property. Investors should look for properties that are priced below market value to ensure they have room to make a profit after factoring in rehab costs and other expenses.
4. Additionally, investors should consider the **potential resale value** of the property after the rehab is complete. Properties that have the potential to sell for significantly more than the purchase price plus rehab costs are ideal for fix and flip investments.

5.2 Identifying the Best Markets for Fix and Flip Investing

In addition to understanding the criteria for profitable fix and flip properties, investors must also identify the best markets for fix and flip investing. While there is no one-size-fits-all answer to this question, there are certain characteristics that tend to make a market more favorable for fix and flip investors. These include **high demand** for housing, **low inventory**, and a **growing economy** with strong job growth and population growth.

Another important factor to consider is the **level of competition** in the market. Investors should look for markets with relatively low competition to ensure they have a better chance of finding undervalued properties and making profitable deals.

Additionally, investors should research the local real estate market to determine the *average sale price*, *days on market*, and other *key metrics* that can help them make informed decisions about which properties to invest in.

5.3 Strategies for Finding and Analyzing Fix and Flip Properties

Once investors have identified the best markets for fix and flip investing, the next step is to find and analyze potential properties. There are several strategies that investors can use to find properties, including:

1. working with real estate agents,
2. attending auctions,
3. searching online listings, and
4. marketing directly to distressed property owners.

Once potential properties have been identified, investors should **conduct a thorough analysis** to determine whether they meet the criteria for a profitable fix and flip project. This analysis should include:

1. an assessment of the property's condition,
2. rehab costs,
3. resale value,
4. potential profit margins, and

5. holding costs, such as property taxes, insurance, and utilities.

5.4 Tips for Evaluating Property Condition and Rehab Costs

Evaluating property condition and estimating rehab costs is a critical aspect of the fix and flip investment process. Investors should **conduct a thorough inspection** of the property to identify any *structural issues*, *water damage*, or other problems that could impact the cost of rehabbing the property. They should also obtain **multiple bids from contractors** to ensure they have an accurate estimate of the rehab costs.

Investors should also consider the **potential return on investment** when evaluating rehab costs. While it may be tempting to cut corners and choose cheaper materials or methods, investors should prioritize quality and long-term value to maximize profits. This means using **high-quality materials** that will last, investing in energy-efficient upgrades, and ensuring that the property meets all local building codes and regulations.

In addition to evaluating property condition and rehab costs, investors should also consider the **timeline for completing the rehab project**. Time is money in the fix and flip business, so investors should aim to complete the project as quickly as possible to *minimize holding costs* and *maximize profits*. This requires careful planning and project management to ensure that all tasks are completed efficiently and on schedule.

5.5 How to Make Offers and Negotiate Deals for Fix and Flip Properties

Once investors have found a potential fix and flip property and conducted a thorough analysis, the next step is to **make an offer** and **negotiate the deal**. This can be a complex and challenging process, particularly for investors who are new to the fix and flip business. Some tips for making offers and negotiating deals include:

- **Start with a low offer:** Investors should always start with a low offer to leave room for negotiation. This can help them secure a better deal and maximize profits.
- **Be prepared to walk away:** If negotiations are not going well or the deal does not meet the investor's criteria, it may be best to walk away and look for other opportunities.
- **Understand the seller's motivations:** Understanding the seller's motivations can help investors make more effective offers and negotiate better deals. For example, if the seller is motivated to sell quickly, investors may be able to secure a lower purchase price.
- **Use contingencies wisely:** Contingencies can be useful tools for protecting investors in case of unexpected issues or problems with the property. However, investors should use them wisely to avoid scaring off sellers or making the deal too complicated.

Conclusion

Finding profitable fix and flip properties requires careful research, analysis, and due diligence. Investors must understand the criteria for profitable properties, identify the best markets for fix and flip investing, and use effective strategies for finding and analyzing potential properties. They must also be skilled at evaluating property condition and rehab costs, making offers and negotiating deals, and managing rehab projects efficiently to maximize profits. With the right knowledge, skills, and strategies, investors can achieve success in the fix and flip business and generate significant returns on their investments.

Chapter 6: Property Valuation Strategies for Fix and Flip Investing

Property valuation is an essential aspect of real estate investing, and it is particularly critical in fix and flip investing. Accurate valuation ensures that you buy the property at the right price and sell it for a profit. This chapter will provide a comprehensive overview of property valuation strategies for fix and flip investing, including the basics of property valuation, the different approaches to valuing properties, identifying key factors that affect property values, evaluating and analyzing property values, and best practices for accurately valuing fix and flip properties.

6.1 Basics of Property Valuation in Real Estate Investing

Property valuation is the process of determining the value of a property based on a variety of factors, including *location*, *condition*, *size*, and *amenities*. The value of a property can be influenced by external factors such as the *local housing market*, *economic conditions*, and *interest rates*.

Real estate investors use different methods to value properties, including the *market approach*, *income approach*, and *cost approach*.

The goal of property valuation is to determine the **fair market value** of a property, which is the price a buyer is willing to pay and a seller is willing to accept in an open and competitive market.

By understanding the methods of property valuation and the factors that influence the fair market value of a property, real estate investors can make informed decisions about buying, selling, and managing properties.

6.2 Understanding the Different Approaches to Valuing Properties

Real estate investors use several methods to value properties, including the market approach, income approach, and cost approach.

1. **Market Approach:** This approach to property valuation involves comparing the property being valued to **similar properties** in the area that have recently sold. This method is based on the principle of supply and demand and assumes that buyers will pay a similar price for similar properties in the same area. The market approach is ideal for valuing residential properties and is often used by real estate agents to determine the listing price of a property.
2. **Income Approach:** This method is used to value commercial and rental properties. It involves determining the net operating income (NOI) of the property, which is the income generated from the property after deducting expenses such as taxes, maintenance, and management fees. The NOI is then divided by the capitalization rate (cap rate), which is the rate of return that investors expect from the property. The resulting value represents the property's fair market value.

3. **Cost Approach:** This method involves determining the cost of replacing the property if it were destroyed and then subtracting any depreciation. The cost approach is based on the assumption that a buyer will not pay more for a property than it would cost to build a similar property from scratch. This method is often used to value unique properties that do not have comparable properties in the area.

6.3 Identifying Key Factors that Affect Property Values in Fix and Flip Investing

Several factors can affect the value of a property in fix and flip investing, including location, condition, size, amenities, and market conditions.

1. **Location** is a critical factor in property valuation, as properties in *desirable neighborhoods* or areas with *strong job growth* and *good schools* tend to command higher prices.
2. The **condition** of the property is also an important factor in property valuation, as properties that require extensive renovations or repairs may have lower values.
3. **Size and amenities** such as the number of bedrooms and bathrooms, the *size of the lot*, and the presence of a *pool* or *garage* can also impact property values.
4. **Market conditions** such as *interest rates*, *housing inventory*, and *economic conditions* can also affect property values. In a strong housing market with low inventory and high demand, property values may increase, while in a weak housing market with high inventory and low demand, property values may decrease.

6.4 How to Evaluate and Analyze Property Values for Better Investment Decisions

Evaluating and analyzing property values is a critical step in making better investment decisions in fix and flip investing.

1. The first step is to research the **local housing market** to understand *market trends*, *inventory*, and *demand.*
2. Next, you should conduct a **comparative market analysis** (CMA) to determine the fair market value of the subject property. This involves comparing the subject property to *similar properties* that have recently sold in the same area.
3. You should also **inspect the property** thoroughly to identify any issues that could impact its value. This includes assessing the *condition of the property*, evaluating any necessary *repairs or renovations*, and estimating the *cost of these repairs.*
4. Finally, you should factor in all of the **costs** associated with the project, including the *purchase price*, *renovation costs*, and *holding costs*, to arrive at an accurate estimate of the potential profit margin.

6.5 Best Practices for Accurately Valuing Fix and Flip Properties

To accurately value fix and flip properties, it is essential to follow best practices.

1. One of the most important practices is to use **reliable data sources** for your research, including *real estate websites*, *public records*, and *local market reports.*
2. Additionally, it is crucial to conduct a **thorough inspection** of the property and to bring in experts, such as *home inspectors* or *contractors*, to identify any issues that could impact the value.

3. It is also essential to be **realistic** in your **valuation**, taking into account all of the costs associated with the project, including *renovation costs*, *holding costs*, and *transaction costs*.
4. Finally, it is critical to stay up-to-date on **market trends and conditions**, as these can have a significant impact on property values.

By staying informed and using best practices for property valuation, you can make better investment decisions and increase your chances of success in fix and flip investing.

Conclusion

Property valuation is a critical aspect of fix and flip investing, and accurate valuation is essential for buying properties at the right price and selling them for a profit. By understanding the different approaches to valuing properties, identifying key factors that affect property values, and following best practices for property valuation, you can make better investment decisions and increase your chances of success in fix and flip investing. Remember to conduct thorough research, inspect the property thoroughly, be realistic in your valuation, and stay up-to-date on market trends and conditions. With these strategies in place, you can accurately value fix and flip properties and achieve success in real estate investing.

Chapter 7: Negotiation Strategies for Fix and Flip Investing

Negotiation - Photo by Gabrielle Henderson

Negotiation is an essential part of fix and flip investing, as investors must negotiate with sellers, buyers, contractors, and other parties to ensure that they get the best possible deal on a property. This chapter will discuss the basics of negotiation in real estate investing and provide strategies and techniques for successful negotiations.

7.1 Basics of Negotiation in Real Estate Investing

Negotiation in real estate investing involves two parties with different interests coming together to reach a mutually beneficial agreement. The goal of the negotiation is to *create a win-win outcome*, where both parties feel satisfied with the deal. Negotiation skills are essential for fix and flip investors, as they often negotiate with multiple parties, including sellers, buyers, and contractors.

1. One of the most important skills in negotiation is

communication. Successful negotiation requires clear and effective communication between parties. Fix and flip investors must be able to *listen actively* to the other party and express their interests and concerns clearly.

2. Another key aspect of negotiation is **preparation**. Fix and flip investors must *research* the property and the other party before entering into negotiations. Understanding the property's value and the *other party's motivations* and interests can help investors negotiate more effectively.

7.2 Key Negotiation Strategies for Fix and Flip Investors

Fix and flip investors can benefit from utilizing several key negotiation strategies to increase their chances of success in their real estate deals.

1. One important strategy is to **focus on interests** rather than positions. This means that instead of simply staking out a specific position, such as a particular price point, investors should take the time to *understand the underlying motivations and goals* of the other party involved in the negotiation. By doing this, fix and flip investors can identify opportunities to **create a win-win** outcome that meets both parties' interests. For example, a seller may be motivated by a desire to sell quickly, while a fix and flip investor may be looking for a property at a lower price point. By understanding each other's interests, the two parties can work together to come up with a solution that benefits both.
2. Another key negotiation strategy for fix and flip investors is to **set clear objectives** and priorities before entering into negotiations. This means determining in advance what their *bottom line* is, which represents the *minimum acceptable outcome*, and what their *walk-away point* is, which is the point at which they are no longer willing to continue negotiations.

By having a clear understanding of these objectives, investors can stay focused on their goals and avoid making rash decisions that could lead to unfavorable outcomes.

3. Lastly, fix and flip investors should be willing to **compromise and be flexible** in their negotiations. This means being *open to creative solutions* that meet both parties' interests and being willing to make concessions to reach an agreement. For example, a fix and flip investor may be willing to accept a higher purchase price if the seller agrees to extend the closing date or make necessary repairs to the property.

Being flexible and willing to negotiate can help fix and flip investors build positive relationships with other parties involved in the transaction, which can be beneficial in future deals.

7.3 Understanding the Other Party's Motivations and Interests

In any negotiation, understanding the other party's motivations and interests is a critical component to achieving a successful outcome. This is especially true for fix and flip investors who are often dealing with multiple parties, such as *sellers*, *contractors*, and *lenders*. By researching and understanding the other party's motivations and interests, fix and flip investors can identify opportunities to create a mutually beneficial agreement.

1. One effective way to understand the other party's motivations is to **ask open-ended questions** and **listen actively** to their responses. This involves asking questions that require more than a simple "yes" or "no" answer, and instead, encourage the other party to share their *thoughts*, *feelings*, and *concerns*. This approach can help investors identify the other party's **needs** and **interests**, which they can use to find

common ground and negotiate a deal that meets both parties' interests.

2. Another important strategy for understanding the other party's motivations is to **build rapport** and **establish a relationship** with them. This involves creating a positive and productive negotiation environment where both parties feel comfortable sharing their interests and concerns. This can be accomplished by being *respectful and courteous*, *demonstrating empathy*, and showing a *willingness to collaborate* and find solutions together.
3. Fix and flip investors may also want to **do some research** on the other party to gain a deeper understanding of their *motivations and interests*. This could include *reviewing public records*, such as property ownership or legal filings, as well as conducting *interviews with other people* who have worked with the other party in the past.

In summary, understanding the other party's motivations and interests is critical for successful negotiations. Fix and flip investors can use a combination of strategies, such as asking open-ended questions, building rapport, and conducting research, to gain a deeper understanding of the other party and negotiate a deal that meets both parties' interests.

7.4 Techniques for Overcoming Negotiation Barriers and Deadlocks

When negotiations hit a deadlock or barriers arise, it can be challenging for fix and flip investors to achieve their desired outcomes. However, with the right techniques, it is possible to overcome these challenges and find a way forward.

1. One effective technique for overcoming negotiation barriers

is to **brainstorm together** to generate creative solutions that meet both parties' interests. This involves *generating as many potential solutions* as possible without evaluating them initially. Once all the ideas have been generated, the parties evaluate them and choose the one that works best for both parties. This approach can help break down the barriers that prevent agreement and can lead to new and innovative solutions that neither party may have considered previously.

2. Another strategy for overcoming negotiation barriers is to just explore **different options and find alternatives** that both parties can agree on. This involves being *open-minded* and *willing to explore* multiple potential solutions. Fix and flip investors can encourage the other party to express their concerns and needs, and then work collaboratively to identify possible alternatives that address those needs. By doing so, both parties can achieve their goals and find common ground.
3. Finally, it's important to find common ground and **build on areas of agreement** to overcome negotiation barriers. Fix and flip investors should focus on areas where both parties share similar interests and try to find ways to build on those areas to create a mutually beneficial agreement. For example, if both parties agree that a quick closing is important, the investor could offer to waive certain contingencies or negotiate a higher purchase price in exchange for a quicker closing. This approach can help to find solutions that benefit both parties and help overcome the barriers that prevent agreement.

In summary, overcoming negotiation barriers and deadlocks requires **creativity**, **open-mindedness**, and a willingness to find **common ground**. By using techniques such as brainstorming, exploring different options, and building on areas of agreement, fix and flip investors can overcome negotiation barriers and achieve their desired outcomes.

7.5 How to Close the Deal and Create a Win-Win Outcome

Closing the deal and creating a win-win outcome is the ultimate goal of any negotiation, and this is especially true for fix and flip investors. To achieve this goal, it is important to ensure that both parties feel satisfied with the agreement and that all the details and terms are clearly spelled out in writing.

1. One key strategy for achieving a win-win outcome is to **use various negotiation techniques** that help overcome any barriers and deadlocks that may arise during the negotiation process. *Compromise* is one such technique, where both parties agree to a solution that partially satisfies each party's interests. Another technique is *collaboration*, where both parties work together to find a solution that meets the needs of both parties.
2. In addition to these techniques, fix and flip investors should have a clear understanding of their **goals and objectives**. This means identifying their bottom line, or the minimum acceptable outcome, and their walk-away point, or the point at which they are no longer willing to continue the negotiation. By having a clear understanding of their objectives, fix and flip investors can stay focused on their goals and avoid making rash decisions.
3. Finally, it is important for fix and flip investors to be **willing to be flexible** and creative in order to find a solution that works for both parties. This means being *open to new ideas*, considering all the options available, and being willing to make concessions in order to reach an agreement. By doing

so, fix and flip investors can create a win-win outcome that benefits everyone involved.

In summary, closing the deal and creating a win-win outcome requires a combination of negotiation techniques, a clear understanding of goals and objectives, and a willingness to be flexible and creative. By utilizing these strategies, fix and flip investors can successfully negotiate a deal that meets both parties' interests and leads to a mutually beneficial agreement.

Conclusion

In conclusion, negotiation is a critical skill for fix and flip investors. By understanding the basics of negotiation, using key strategies, understanding the other party's motivations and interests, and utilizing techniques to overcome barriers and deadlocks, fix and flip investors can successfully negotiate deals that create a win-win outcome for all parties involved.

Chapter 8: Financing Your Fix and Flip Project

Financing - Photo by Karolina Grabowska

When it comes to real estate investing, fix and flip projects can be both profitable and exciting. However, financing these projects can be a daunting task. In this chapter, we will discuss the different types of financing options available for fix and flip investors, how to qualify for these options, creative financing strategies, strategies for negotiating financing terms, and how to choose the right lender. We will also cover how to manage your fix and flip budget and cash flow effectively.

8.1 Understanding the Different Types of Financing Options for Fix and Flip Investing

There are several financing options available for fix and flip investors, including traditional bank loans, private money loans and hard money loans.

Traditional Bank Loans: Traditional bank loans are one of the most common financing options for fix and flip investors. They typically offer *lower interest rates* and *longer repayment terms* than other financing options. However, traditional bank loans *require good credit, a solid business plan*, and a *track record of successful real estate projects*. The application process for traditional bank loans can be lengthy and require a lot of paperwork.

Private Money Loans: Private money loans are *offered by individuals or groups*, such as friends, family members, or acquaintances. Private money loans are typically *easier to qualify* for than bank loans because they are based on personal relationships and trust. Private money loans also offer *more flexibility in terms* of repayment terms and interest rates. However, private money loans may come with *higher interest rates* than traditional bank loans.

Hard Money Loans: Hard money loans are *short-term loans* offered by private lenders that are secured by the property itself. Hard money loans are typically *easier to qualify* for than traditional bank loans and can be *obtained more quickly*. Hard money loans come with *higher interest rates* than traditional bank loans because they are considered higher-risk loans due to their short-term nature and lack of collateral. Hard money loans are often used by fix and flip investors who need quick financing to purchase a property and make necessary repairs before selling it.

Summary

1. **Traditional bank loans** offer *lower interest rates* and *longer repayment terms*, but they are harder to qualify for and require a lot of paperwork.
2. **Private money loans** and **hard money loans** have *higher interest rates*, but they are *easier to qualify for* and can be

obtained more quickly than traditional bank loans.

8.2 Qualifying for Fix and Flip Financing

Qualifying for financing is a critical step in any fix and flip project, and it can make the difference between success and failure. When applying for financing, the lender will evaluate several factors to determine whether you are a good candidate for the loan. These factors may vary depending on the type of loan you are applying for, but some of the most common ones include *credit score*, *income*, *assets*, and *experience*.

Traditional bank loans are typically the *most difficult to qualify for*, as they require a *high credit score* (usually at least 680) and a *solid business plan*. They may also require a track record of *successful real estate projects*, which can be difficult for new investors who are just starting out. In addition, traditional bank loans may have a *longer application process* and *require more paperwork* than other financing options.

Private money lenders and hard money lenders, on the other hand, are more concerned with the *value of the property* and the *potential profit* than your credit score or income.

1. **Private money lenders** are typically individuals or groups who lend money to real estate investors based on the value of the property and the potential for a profitable return on investment.
2. **Hard money lenders** are similar, but they typically *charge higher interest rates* and require a down payment and proof of income or assets.

To increase your chances of qualifying for financing, it's important to have a **solid business plan** that outlines your project's goals, timelines, and budgets. You should also have a good understanding of the **local**

real estate market and be able to demonstrate the **potential for a profitable return** on investment. Additionally, having **experience in real estate investing** can be a major advantage when applying for financing, as it shows lenders that you have a track record of success and are less risky to invest in. If you are new to real estate investing, consider partnering with an experienced investor or seeking out mentorship to build your skills and increase your chances of success.

8.3 Creative Financing Strategies for Fix and Flip Projects

There are several creative financing strategies that fix and flip investors can use to finance their projects.

1. **Partnering with other investors** or **real estate professionals** can be a great option for fix and flip investors who may not have the necessary capital or expertise to finance and execute the project on their own. This strategy can involve forming a *joint venture* where each party contributes capital, resources, or expertise in exchange for a share of the profits. Another option is to work with a **silent partner** who provides the necessary capital in exchange for a percentage of the profits, without being involved in the day-to-day operations of the project.
2. Using a **home equity line of credit (HELOC)** is another option for financing a fix and flip project. HELOCs allow homeowners to borrow against the equity in their homes, and can provide a flexible and low-interest option for financing the project. However, this strategy does come with some risks, as it involves using your own home as collateral. If the project does not go as planned and you are unable to repay the loan, you could potentially lose your home.
3. Negotiating a **seller carryback** is a strategy that can be used when the seller of the property is motivated and willing to

work with the buyer to finance part or all of the purchase price of the property. This strategy involves the seller financing the purchase, and the buyer making payments to the seller over an agreed-upon period of time. This can be a good option for buyers who may not be able to qualify for traditional financing, or who want to avoid the high interest rates of other financing options.

4. Using **personal loans**, **credit cards**, or **borrowing from friends and family** are other financing options that can be used as a last resort option. However, these options should be used with caution, as they can have *high interest rates* and can strain personal relationships if not repaid in a timely manner. It's important to carefully consider the risks and benefits of these financing options before deciding to use them for a fix and flip project.

8.4 Strategies for Negotiating Financing Terms

When negotiating financing terms for a fix and flip project, it's important to have a solid understanding of your own financial situation as well as the lender's requirements and preferences. Before entering into negotiations, you should have a clear idea of your budget, the amount of financing you need, and the terms you are seeking.

1. To start, it's important to present yourself as a **qualified borrower**. This means having a good *credit score, a solid business plan*, and a *track record of successful real estate projects.* Lenders want to see that you have experience and the ability to execute your plan. If you're new to fix and flip projects, consider *partnering* with someone who has more experience to help improve your credibility.
2. When negotiating with lenders, be sure to *understand all of the terms of the loan*, including the *interest rate, repayment*

period, and any *fees or penalties*. Ask questions and don't be afraid to negotiate for better terms. For example, you may be able to negotiate a lower interest rate by offering a larger down payment or by showing that you have additional assets to secure the loan.

3. Another strategy for negotiating financing terms is to **shop around and compare offers** from different lenders. You can use online comparison tools or **work with a mortgage broker** to find the best deal. This can help you find the best rate and give you leverage when negotiating with lenders. Just be sure to compare apples to apples, as some lenders may offer lower rates but have higher fees or penalties.
4. Finally, it's important to be **honest and transparent with lenders.** Don't try to hide any potential problems or risks associated with your project, as this will only hurt your chances of getting financing. Instead, be upfront about any challenges and work with the lender to find solutions that meet both your needs. Being honest and transparent can help build trust with lenders and increase your chances of getting the financing you need.

8.5 How to Choose the Right Lender for Your Fix and Flip Project

Choosing the right lender is critical to the success of your fix and flip project.

1. **Experience:** When looking for a lender, consider their *experience with fix and flip projects*. You want to work with a lender who has experience in this area and understands the unique challenges and risks associated with it. An experienced lender can help you navigate potential pitfalls and provide valuable insights that can increase your chances

of success.

2. **Reputation:** Checking the lender's reputation is important. You can look at *online reviews* and *references* from other real estate investors in your network. Consider the lender's *track record* and whether they have a history of working well with other investors.
3. **Interest rates:** Compare interest rates from multiple lenders to ensure you are getting the best deal possible. Keep in mind that interest rates can vary depending on factors such as your credit score and the loan-to-value ratio of the property. It's important to consider the *overall cost* of the loan, including the interest rate and any fees or penalties.
4. **Fees and penalties:** Ask about any fees or penalties associated with the loan, such as *prepayment penalties* or *origination fees*. Make sure you understand all of the costs involved before agreeing to the loan. You don't want to be surprised by unexpected fees or penalties that can eat into your profits.
5. **Repayment terms:** Look for lenders who offer *flexible repayment terms* that fit your budget and timeline. Consider factors such as the *length of the repayment period*, whether the loan is *interest-only* or fully amortized, and whether there are any *balloon payments*. You want to make sure the loan terms align with your project goals and financial needs.
6. **Responsiveness:** Choose a lender who is responsive and easy to work with. The lender should be willing to *answer your questions* and *provide support* throughout the project. You don't want to work with a lender who is *difficult to communicate* with or unresponsive when you need help.

Overall, it's important to do your research and consider these factors when choosing a lender for your fix and flip project. By choosing the right lender, you can increase your chances of success and achieve your financial goals.

8.6 Managing Your Fix and Flip Budget and Cash Flow

Here are some additional details on managing your fix and flip budget and cash flow:

1. **Create a detailed budget:** Your budget should include all of the costs associated with the project, such as the *purchase price*, *renovation costs*, *closing costs*, and *holding costs*. You should also include a **contingency fund** for unexpected expenses. Make sure to research the costs of materials and labor in your area and factor in any necessary permits or inspections.
2. **Track expenses:** You should track your expenses carefully to ensure that you stay on budget. Use a spreadsheet or accounting software to *record all of your expenses* and *keep receipts* for all purchases. *Review your budget regularly* to make sure you are on track and adjust it as needed.
3. **Create a financing timeline:** Your timeline should outline the *major milestones* of the project, such as when you *plan to purchase the property*, *start and complete renovations*, and *list the property for sale*. This will help you stay on track and ensure that you complete the project within your budget and timeline.
4. **Plan for repayment:** You should have a solid plan for repaying your loans. This may involve *selling the property* quickly to pay off the loan, *refinancing the loan*, or using other sources of income to repay the loan. Make sure you understand the repayment terms and have a *backup plan* in case your project runs into unexpected challenges or delays.
5. **Monitor your cash flow:** You should monitor your cash flow

carefully throughout the project to ensure that you have enough funds to cover expenses. You should also have a **contingency plan** in case you run into unexpected challenges or delays. It's important to be proactive and take steps to address any issues before they become major problems.

Conclusion

Financing your fix and flip project can be a complex and challenging process, but it's critical to the success of your project. By understanding the different financing options available, qualifying for financing, using creative financing strategies, negotiating financing terms, choosing the right lender, and managing your budget and cash flow effectively, you can increase your chances of success and maximize your profits. Remember to be patient, thorough, and diligent throughout the process, and always be willing to seek advice and support from experienced professionals.

Chapter 9: Planning and Executing Your Fix and Flip Project

Planning - Photo by airfocus

Fix and flip investing can be a profitable real estate investment strategy, but it requires careful planning and execution. A successful fix and flip project involves finding the right property, creating a realistic budget, and managing the renovation process effectively. In this chapter, we'll discuss the key steps involved in planning and executing a fix and flip project, from developing a comprehensive project plan and timeline to managing the day-to-day operations and dealing with common challenges.

9.1 Developing a Comprehensive Project Plan and Timeline

Developing a comprehensive project plan and timeline for a fix and flip project involves several key steps.

1. **Define the scope of work:** The first step in developing a

project plan and timeline is to define the *scope of work* required for the project. This means creating a detailed list of all the *renovations*, *repairs*, and *upgrades* needed for the property. The list should be comprehensive and based on a thorough inspection of the property. The scope of work should be specific and include details about the materials and labor needed for each task.

2. **Prioritize tasks:** Once the scope of work is defined, investors should prioritize the tasks according to their *importance*, *difficulty*, and *cost*. This will help ensure that the most critical tasks are completed first, and that the budget is allocated appropriately. For example, it may be more important to address foundational issues than cosmetic upgrades.
3. **Create a timeline:** Based on the scope of work and task prioritization, investors should create a timeline for the project. This timeline should include *each phase of the renovation*, along with *specific milestones* and *deadlines*. It should also take into account any *permits*, *inspections*, or other *regulatory requirements* that may affect the project. The timeline should be as detailed as possible, including specific dates for tasks like electrical or plumbing work.
4. **Allocate resources:** Investors should allocate resources, such as *labor*, *materials*, and *equipment*, according to the timeline. This will help to ensure that the right resources are available at the right time, and that the project stays on track. For example, if the project requires a specific type of flooring, it should be ordered and delivered in time for installation.
5. **Consider contingency plans:** Finally, investors should consider contingency plans for unexpected delays, changes, or challenges that may arise during the project. This could include *building in extra time or budget* for unforeseen circumstances, or having *backup resources* available if needed.

For example, if there is a delay in receiving materials, there should be a backup plan for how to continue work while waiting.

By following these steps, investors can create a detailed project plan and timeline that takes into account all the necessary factors for a successful fix and flip project.

9.2 Creating a Realistic Budget for Your Fix and Flip Project

One of the most critical aspects of a fix and flip project is creating a realistic budget (see Section 8.6).

1. Investors should carefully **consider all of the costs** involved in the project, including *acquisition costs*, *renovation costs*, and *closing costs*. It's also important to factor in a *contingency fund* to cover unexpected expenses that may arise during the renovation process.
2. To create a realistic budget, investors should **work closely with their contractor** and other members of their team to develop a detailed *list of the materials and supplies* needed for the renovation.
3. Investors should also **shop around** for the *best prices on materials and supplies* and *negotiate with contractors* to get the best possible price for their services.

By creating a realistic budget and sticking to it, investors can maximize their profits and minimize their risks.

9.3 Finding and Hiring the Right Contractors for Your Project

Finding and hiring the right contractors for a fix and flip project can be a challenging and time-consuming process:

1. **Ask for referrals and do research:** One way to find potential contractors is to ask for *referrals* from other real estate investors, industry professionals, or friends and family who have had successful experiences with contractors. Investors can also *research local contractors online*, through *professional associations*, or by checking with the Better Business Bureau.
2. **Check references and credentials:** Once investors have a list of potential contractors, they should check their references and credentials. This includes *asking for references* from previous clients and *checking their licensing and insurance status*.
3. **Interview multiple candidates:** Investors should interview multiple candidates to find the contractor who best fits their project and goals. During the interview process, they should ask about the *contractor's experience*, their approach to the project, and their availability and responsiveness.
4. **Review previous work:** Investors should also review the contractor's portfolio of previous work to ensure that they have experience with *similar projects* and that their work meets the investor's standards.
5. **Get written estimates and contracts:** Once investors have selected a contractor, they should get written estimates that outline the scope of the work, the timeline, and the payment schedule. They should also have a *written contract* that includes these details, as well as any warranties, guarantees, or other terms.
6. **Communicate regularly:** Communication is key to a

successful contractor-investor relationship. Investors should maintain regular communication with their contractor to ensure that the project is progressing according to plan and to address any issues that may arise.

By taking these steps and finding and hiring the right contractors for their fix and flip project, investors can ensure that the renovation work is done to a high standard and that the project stays on track and within budget.

9.4 Managing the Day-to-Day Operations of Your Fix and Flip Project

In order to manage the day-to-day operations of a fix and flip project effectively, here are some additional details on what investors should consider:

Communication

- Encourage open communication with the entire team, including contractors, subcontractors, and suppliers. This ensures that everyone is aware of any changes, updates, or issues that may arise during the project.
- Use technology to facilitate communication, such as project management software or messaging apps. This can help streamline communication and ensure that everyone is kept up-to-date.

Schedule

- Develop a detailed schedule that includes *deadlines*, *milestones*, and *specific tasks* to be completed each day or week.

- *Regularly review and update* the schedule to ensure that it is still feasible and on track to meet the project's goals.

Budget

- Develop a comprehensive budget that includes all anticipated costs, including *materials*, *labor*, *permits*, and any other expenses related to the project.
- Monitor the budget closely and make adjustments as needed. This can help to prevent cost overruns and ensure that there is enough funding available to complete the project.

Quality Control

- Conduct regular *site visits* to monitor the quality of the work being done. This can help identify any issues or concerns early on, allowing for prompt resolution.
- Review *inspection reports* and other quality control measures to ensure that the work is being done to the appropriate standards.

Documentation

- Create a system for organizing and storing project-related documents, such as *invoices*, *contracts*, *permits*, and *receipts*.
- Make sure that all team members are aware of the system and know how to access the documents as needed.

Overall, effective project management is essential for the success of a fix and flip project. By staying organized, communicating regularly, and monitoring progress, investors can ensure that their project stays on track and is completed successfully.

9.5 Dealing with Common Challenges in Fix and Flip Rehab Projects

Despite careful planning and execution, fix and flip rehab projects can encounter a variety of challenges.

1. **Unexpected Expenses**

- During a fix and flip project, investors may encounter unexpected expenses that can significantly impact the project's budget and timeline. These expenses can be due to *unforeseen damages*, *code violations*, or any other *unexpected costs*.
- To mitigate this, it's important for investors to set aside a *contingency budget* of at least 10-20% of the total project cost. This contingency budget should be included in the project's budget plan and should be used to cover any unexpected expenses that may arise during the project.
- Additionally, investors should *review expenses regularly* and adjust the budget as needed to account for unexpected costs. Keeping detailed records of expenses can help investors identify any areas where the budget may need to be adjusted.

1. **Delays**

- Delays are another common challenge that investors may face during a fix and flip project. Delays can occur due to various reasons, including *inclement weather*, *supply chain disruptions*, or unexpected issues that arise during the project.
- To deal with delays, investors should build in some flexibility in the project timeline and be prepared to adjust the schedule as needed. This can include *setting realistic timelines* and

regularly reviewing the project schedule to ensure that the project is on track.

- Clear *communication with contractors and team members* is also important to ensure that everyone is aware of any delays and can adjust their plans accordingly. By maintaining open lines of communication, investors can quickly address any issues that may arise and minimize the impact of delays on the project.

1. **Contractor Issues**

- Contractor issues can include *delays in completing work*, *poor quality work*, or *disputes over payment*. These issues can significantly impact the project's budget and timeline, and can also strain the working relationship between investors and contractors.
- To minimize these issues, investors should *choose contractors carefully* and make sure to have a *written contract in place* that outlines expectations and payment schedules. This can help ensure that both parties are on the same page and can help avoid any misunderstandings or disputes.
- *Regular communication* with contractors is also important to address any issues as they arise and maintain a positive working relationship. By maintaining open lines of communication, investors can quickly address any issues that may arise and help ensure that the project stays on track.

1. **Permitting Issues**

- Permitting issues can also pose a challenge during a fix and flip project. These issues can arise due to various reasons, including *missing permits*, *changes in building codes*, or *delays in obtaining permits.*

- To minimize these issues, investors should make sure to obtain all necessary permits and approvals *before beginning work*. This can include working with local officials to ensure that the project meets all requirements and that all necessary permits and approvals are obtained.
- It's also important to regularly review the project's *compliance with building codes and regulations* to avoid any potential fines or penalties. By staying up-to-date with regulations and requirements, investors can help ensure that the project stays on track and complies with all relevant regulations.

By being proactive and flexible, investors can overcome common challenges and ensure the success of their fix and flip project.

Conclusion

Planning and executing a fix and flip project requires careful attention to detail and effective project management skills. By developing a comprehensive project plan and timeline, creating a realistic budget, finding and hiring the right contractors, managing the day-to-day operations effectively, and dealing with common challenges, investors can maximize their profits and minimize their risks. With the right approach, fix and flip investing can be a profitable real estate investment strategy for investors of all experience levels.

Chapter 10: Maximizing Your ROI in Fix and Flip Investing

Profit - Photo by Towfiqu barbhuiya

Real estate is a lucrative investment option, but it comes with its own set of challenges. Fix and flip investing, in particular, can be quite profitable, but it requires a certain level of skill and knowledge. This chapter will discuss various strategies that can help maximize your ROI in fix and flip investing. We will start by defining ROI in the context of fix and flip investments.

10.1 Understanding ROI in Fix and Flip Investing

Return on investment (ROI) is a crucial metric for any investment, including fix and flip properties. It is the **percentage of profit earned on the amount invested.** In the case of fix and flip investments, ROI is calculated by subtracting the total cost of the property (purchase price and renovation expenses) from the sale price and dividing the result by the total cost. For example, if you purchase a property for

$200,000, spend $50,000 on renovations, and sell it for $300,000, your ROI would be ((300,000-250,000)/250,000)*100 = 20%.

The ROI calculation should include **all costs** associated with the investment, such as *purchase price*, *renovation expenses*, *holding costs*, *closing costs*, and *selling costs*. Investors should also consider the **time it takes to complete** the project and the potential risks involved, such as *market fluctuations* or unexpected expenses.

A high ROI is desirable for fix and flip investors, but it's important to note that **higher returns usually come with higher risks**. Investors should also consider other factors such as the *local real estate market conditions*, *competition*, and potential *demand* for the property.

Furthermore, it's important to keep in mind that ROI is not the only metric that investors should consider. Other important factors that may impact the success of a fix and flip project include *cash flow*, *capital gains*, and *tax implications*. Investors should take a holistic approach to evaluate the potential returns and risks associated with a fix and flip investment and make informed decisions accordingly.

10.2 Strategies for Maximizing Your Returns in Fix and Flip Projects

There are several strategies you can use to maximize your returns in fix and flip projects.

1. **Buy the right property at the right price:** Conducting thorough market research is key to finding the right property at the right price. You can use online resources such as real estate websites and public records to search for potential properties. Once you identify a property of interest, you should visit the property in person and inspect it thoroughly to identify any potential issues or renovation needs. You

should also research the local real estate market and gather information about the area, such as *demographics*, *employment rates*, and *home values*, to ensure that the property is in a desirable location. Additionally, it's important to have a clear understanding of your budget and the costs associated with renovation, including materials, labor, permits, and any unexpected expenses.

2. **Work with a reliable team of contractors and professionals:** Building a reliable team of contractors and professionals is essential to the success of a fix and flip project. When selecting contractors, it's important to do your due diligence by *checking references*, *verifying licenses* and *insurance*, and *reviewing past work*. You should also get multiple bids to compare prices and ensure that you're getting a fair deal. To establish a clear scope of work, you should create a *detailed renovation plan* that outlines the work to be done, the materials to be used, and the timeline for completion. It's also important to establish a budget and payment schedule and to communicate regularly with your contractors to ensure that the project stays on track.
3. **Partner with a real estate agent:** A good real estate agent can help you find properties that meet your criteria, negotiate deals, and market your property for sale. Look for agents who have experience in the fix and flip market and are familiar with the local real estate market. You should also *ask for references* and *check their online reviews* to ensure that they have a track record of success. To ensure that you and your agent are on the same page, you should establish clear expectations from the beginning and communicate regularly throughout the project. This can include discussing your budget, renovation timeline, and marketing plan for selling the property.

10.3 Tips for Reducing Your Costs and Increasing Your Profits

1. **Creating a detailed budget:** When creating a detailed budget, it's important to have a clear understanding of all the costs associated with the renovation. This includes *material costs*, *labor costs*, *permits*, and *fees*. You should research the cost of materials and labor in your area and get quotes from contractors to help you estimate your costs accurately. Make sure to also include any additional costs, such as *insurance* and *taxes*, in your budget. It's also important to build in a *contingency budget of 10-20%* to account for unexpected expenses, such as repairs or delays.
2. **Prioritizing renovations:** When prioritizing renovations, it's important to focus on those that will *add the most value* to the property. This may include *updates to the kitchen and bathrooms*, adding more *living space*, or improving the *curb appeal* of the property. To determine which renovations will have the most impact, research the local real estate market and speak with real estate agents and contractors. You should also consider the cost of each renovation and prioritize those that will *provide the highest return* on investment.
3. **Doing some of the work yourself:** Doing some of the work yourself can help you save money, but it's important to be *realistic about your abilities* and to carefully consider which tasks you can handle on your own. Tasks that may be suitable for DIY include *painting*, *installing light fixtures*, and *landscaping*. It's important to factor in the *cost of your time* and any *potential mistakes* you may make when deciding which tasks to handle yourself.

10.4 How to Evaluate and Measure Your ROI for Better Investment Decisions

Measuring and evaluating your ROI is crucial for making better investment decisions. It allows you to determine which properties are most profitable and which strategies are working best for you.

Measuring and evaluating your ROI (Return on Investment) is a key step in fix and flip investing.

1. **Keeping track of all expenses:** To accurately calculate your ROI, it's important to keep track of all the expenses related to the property. This includes the *purchase price*, *renovation costs*, *holding costs* (such as property taxes, insurance, and utilities), and *selling costs* (such as real estate agent commissions and closing costs). It's also important to factor in any unexpected expenses that may arise, such as repair costs or delays in the renovation process.
2. **Calculating your ROI:** To calculate your ROI, use the formula: **ROI = (Net Profit / Total Investment) x 100.** Net profit is the total amount you make from the sale of the property, minus all of the expenses associated with *buying*, *renovating*, and *holding the property*. Total investment includes all of the money you put into the property, including the *purchase price*, *renovation costs*, and *holding costs*.
3. **Re-evaluating your strategies:** If you find that your ROI is lower than expected, you can re-evaluate your strategies and make changes accordingly. This may involve adjusting your *renovation budget*, changing your *marketing strategy*, or reconsidering the *types of properties* you invest in. By analyzing your ROI, you can identify areas for improvement and make changes to improve your future returns.
4. **Comparing properties:** Measuring and evaluating your ROI

also allows you to compare different properties and determine which ones are the most profitable. By comparing the ROI of different properties, you can *identify the best investment opportunities* and make informed decisions about which properties to invest in.

10.5 Building a Profitable Fix and Flip Business

Building a profitable fix and flip business requires patience, persistence, and a solid strategy.

1. **Setting clear investment goals:** Before starting any investment, you should have a clear understanding of what you want to achieve. Determine what your *financial goals* are, whether it's to generate *passive income*, build *wealth over time*, or achieve a *specific ROI*. These goals will help guide your investment strategy and ensure that you are making decisions that align with your overall vision.
2. **Creating a plan:** Once you have set clear investment goals, create a plan for achieving them. This plan should include your *budget*, timeline, and *target ROI*. Your budget should take into account all costs associated with the investment, including *purchase price*, *renovation costs*, and any *holding costs*. Your timeline should include the *expected time* it will take to complete the renovation and sell the property. And your target ROI should reflect your overall financial goals.
3. **Looking for properties:** After creating a plan, start looking for properties that meet your criteria. *Networking* with other investors and real estate professionals can be a great way to find opportunities. You can also *search online* for properties or work with a real estate agent who specializes in fix and flip investments.
4. **Evaluating properties:** When evaluating properties, consider

the *potential for renovation* and the *resale value of the property*. Look for properties that are in *good locations* and have the potential to be improved with renovations. It's important to conduct a thorough inspection of the property to identify any potential issues that could affect the renovation process and the resale value.

5. **Diversifying investments:** As you build your portfolio, diversify your investments by investing in properties in *different locations*, with *different renovation* needs, and at *different price points*. This can help minimize risk and maximize returns over the long term. However, make sure to carefully evaluate each property before investing to ensure it aligns with your investment goals and strategy.

Conclusion

Maximizing your ROI in fix and flip investing requires a combination of knowledge, skill, and strategy. By understanding ROI and implementing strategies to maximize returns, reduce costs, and evaluate investments, you can build a fix and flip business. Remember to be patient, persistent, and willing to adapt your strategies as needed. With the right approach, fix and flip investing can be a lucrative and rewarding investment option.

Chapter 11: Managing Your Time and Resources for Fix and Flip Investing

Time Management - Photo by Aron Visuals

Time management and resource allocation are essential elements of success in any business venture, including fix and flip investing. Fix and flip investors are individuals or companies that purchase undervalued properties, renovate them, and sell them at a profit. The process involves several stages, including property acquisition, renovation, and resale, and each step requires careful planning, organization, and management. In this chapter, we will explore strategies for managing time and resources effectively to achieve success in fix and flip investing.

11.1 Time Management Strategies for Fix and Flip Investors

Effective time management is essential for any business venture, and fix and flip investing is no exception.

1. Creating a **detailed project timeline** involves breaking down

the renovation process into smaller tasks, *estimating the time* required to complete each task, and *setting deadlines* for each task. This helps to ensure that the project stays on schedule, and the investor can anticipate any potential delays and adjust the timeline accordingly. It also helps to allocate resources effectively, such as scheduling contractors to work on specific tasks during specific time frames.

2. **Delegating tasks** to team members or contractors is another effective time management strategy. It allows the investor to focus on their strengths and delegate tasks that they may not be as skilled in, or tasks that are not critical to the success of the project. This approach also enables the investor to *leverage the expertise of team members* or *contractors*, resulting in a more efficient and effective project.
3. **Leveraging technology** is also critical for fix and flip investors. Project management software can help investors track the progress of the project, set reminders for upcoming deadlines, and communicate with team members or contractors efficiently. Time tracking software can help investors monitor their time spent on various tasks, identify areas where time is being wasted, and make necessary adjustments to increase productivity.

In summary, effective time management strategies for fix and flip investors involve creating a detailed project timeline, delegating tasks to team members or contractors, and leveraging technology to streamline processes and improve productivity. By implementing these strategies, fix and flip investors can maximize their efficiency and profitability.

11.2 Prioritizing Tasks and Projects for Maximum Efficiency

Prioritizing tasks and projects is a critical skill for fix and flip investors. Investors must prioritize tasks based on their importance and urgency, which helps them stay focused and productive.

1. One effective way to prioritize tasks is to use the **Eisenhower matrix** which is a popular productivity tool that helps individuals prioritize their tasks by urgency and importance. It divides tasks into four categories:

- **Important and urgent tasks:** These are tasks that require immediate attention and have significant consequences if not completed quickly, such as a property emergency that needs to be addressed.
- **Important but not urgent tasks: These** are tasks that are important but do not require immediate attention, such as planning for future renovation projects or networking with potential investors.
- **Urgent but not important tasks:** These are tasks that are time-sensitive but do not contribute significantly to the overall goals of the project, such as responding to non-critical emails or phone calls.
- **Neither important nor urgent tasks:** These are tasks that do not contribute to the overall goals of the project and can be delegated or eliminated altogether.

1. **Grouping tasks into projects and ranking them by importance** can also help fix and flip investors prioritize their time and resources. For example, an investor may have multiple renovation projects in progress, each with its own timeline and budget. By evaluating each project's *potential*

profitability or *resale value*, the investor can allocate their resources to the projects that are most likely to generate the *highest returns*. Additionally, ranking projects by importance can help the investor focus on *critical projects* first and delegate or postpone less important projects.

11.3 How to Balance Multiple Projects and Investments

Managing multiple projects and investments can be a daunting task for investors. However, there are several effective strategies to help balance multiple projects and ensure that they remain on track to maximize returns.

1. **Delegation:** One of the most effective ways to balance multiple projects is to delegate tasks and responsibilities to a reliable team of contractors or project managers. This approach allows investors to focus on *critical tasks* such as *property acquisition* or *financing* while ensuring that renovation projects stay on track. By delegating tasks, investors can save time and focus on strategic decisions that can increase the overall return on investment.
2. **Communication:** Another important aspect of balancing multiple projects is establishing clear communication channels and project timelines for each project. Clear communication ensures that all team members are *aware of their responsibilities*, *deadlines*, and *budget constraints*. It is crucial to ensure that everyone involved in the projects understands the big picture and is aligned on goals and expectations.
3. **Prioritization:** Prioritizing projects and investments is critical to managing multiple projects effectively. Investors need to identify which projects need immediate attention and which ones can wait. By prioritizing projects, investors

can *allocate resources effectively* and ensure that they are working on the most pressing issues first.

4. **Technology:** Technology can also be useful in balancing multiple projects. Project management software and tools can help investors keep track of project timelines, budgets, and progress. These tools can provide a centralized platform for communication and collaboration and help investors stay on top of the status of each project.

11.4 Managing Your Resources and Budget for Greater Returns

Effective resource and budget management are critical for success in fix and flip investing.

Investors must *manage their resources*, including materials, labor, and time, effectively to ensure that projects are completed on time and within budget.

1. One way to manage resources is to **purchase materials in bulk**, which can help investors save money and reduce the risk of delays due to material shortages.
2. Another way to manage resources is to **hire experienced contractors** who can complete renovation projects efficiently and within budget. Experienced contractors have a better understanding of the renovation process and can provide valuable insights and recommendations to investors, helping them optimize their resources and maximize their returns.

Investors must also *manage their budget effectively* to avoid overspending and ensure profitability.

1. One way to manage the budget is to establish a **detailed project budget** that includes all expenses associated with the

project, such as acquisition costs, renovation costs, marketing costs, and resale fees. Investors can use this budget to track expenses and identify areas where they can reduce costs or reallocate resources.

2. Another way to manage the budget is to **secure financing** that offers *competitive interest rates* and *flexible repayment terms*. Investors can explore various financing options, such as hard money loans, private money loans, or traditional bank loans, to find the best fit for their project and budget.

11.5 Finding a Work-Life Balance as a Fix and Flip Investor

Fix and flip investing can be a time-consuming and demanding venture that requires a significant amount of time and energy. As such, finding a work-life balance can be challenging for fix and flip investors. However, achieving a work-life balance is essential for maintaining physical and mental well-being, avoiding burnout, and improving overall productivity.

1. One way to find a work-life balance is to **establish clear boundaries** between work and personal life. Investors can set specific work hours and allocate time for personal activities, such as *exercise*, *hobbies*, or *spending time with family and friends*. This approach helps investors avoid overworking and maintain a healthy work-life balance.
2. Another way to find a work-life balance is to **delegate tasks and responsibilities** to team members or contractors. Delegation frees up time for investors to focus on personal activities or other business ventures, reducing the risk of burnout and improving overall well-being.

Conclusion

In conclusion, managing time and resources effectively is essential for success in fix and flip investing. Investors must prioritize tasks and projects, delegate responsibilities, and leverage technology to streamline processes and optimize productivity. They must also manage resources and budgets effectively, secure financing, and find a work-life balance to maintain physical and mental well-being. By implementing these strategies, fix and flip investors can maximize their returns and achieve long-term success in the real estate industry

Chapter 12: Marketing and Selling Your Fix and Flip Property

Marketing and selling a fix and flip property is an essential part of the real estate investment process. Effective marketing and selling strategies help investors maximize their return on investment (ROI). In this chapter, we will discuss the importance of marketing in fix and flip investing and how to create a marketing plan for your property. We will also explore the significance of staging and preparing your fix and flip property for sale and how to price and market it for maximum ROI. Additionally, we will delve into leveraging social media and other online channels for property marketing, working with real estate agents to sell your property, and closing the sale to maximize your returns.

12.1 Understanding the Importance of Marketing in Fix and Flip Investing

Marketing is a critical aspect of the fix and flip investing process. It is how investors showcase their property to potential buyers, and it can significantly impact the sale price and return on investment. In today's market, competition is fierce, and investors must stand out to attract buyers. Marketing strategies should *start before the property is even listed for sale*, and investors should have a *clear understanding of their target market*. Here a few strategies to consider:

1. **Identifying Unique Selling Points:** Identifying the unique selling points of a fix and flip property is crucial in developing an effective marketing strategy. Investors need to consider the property's *location*, *size*, *features*, and *quality of the renovation* and use these selling points to attract potential buyers. For example, if the property is located in a desirable neighborhood, investors should highlight this in their marketing materials.
2. **Developing a Comprehensive Marketing Plan:** A comprehensive marketing plan is essential to effectively market a fix and flip property. This plan should include both online and offline marketing strategies. Online marketing strategies may include *social media marketing*, *email marketing*, and *virtual tours*, while offline strategies may include *direct mail*, *open houses*, and *flyers*. Investors should ensure that their marketing materials are consistent and of high quality.
3. **Understanding the Target Market:** Understanding the target market is crucial in developing an effective marketing strategy. Investors should consider the *demographics of potential buyers*, such as *age*, *income level*, and *lifestyle*. This information can help investors tailor their marketing messages and strategies to appeal to their target audience.
4. **High-Quality Photos and Virtual Tours:** High-quality photos and virtual tours of the property are essential in showcasing the property's features and attracting potential buyers. Investors should ensure that their photos are taken by

a *professional photographer* and that the virtual tour is *easy to navigate* and provides an accurate representation of the property.

5. **Importance of Branding:** Branding is an essential aspect of fix and flip investing. A strong brand can *differentiate an investor's properties* from others in the market and create a reputation for quality and value. Investors can develop a brand identity by establishing a *unique logo*, *color scheme*, and *messaging that aligns with their target audience*. *Consistency* in branding across all marketing materials is crucial in establishing a strong brand.

To effectively market a fix and flip property, investors should first identify the property's unique selling points. These can include the property's location, size, features, or the quality of the renovation. Next, investors should develop a comprehensive marketing plan that includes both online and offline marketing strategies. These can include social media marketing, email marketing, direct mail, and open houses. Investors should also have high-quality photos and virtual tours of the property available to potential buyers.

12.2 Creating a Marketing Plan for Your Fix and Flip Property

Creating a marketing plan for a fix and flip property is essential for attracting potential buyers and maximizing ROI. A marketing plan should outline the property's *unique selling points* and *identify the target market*. Once these are established, investors can begin to develop a comprehensive marketing strategy that includes both online and offline marketing efforts.

Online marketing efforts can include social media marketing, email marketing, and online advertising.

1. **Social media marketing** involves creating a social media presence for the property on platforms like Facebook, Instagram, and Twitter. Investors can use these platforms to post high-quality photos and videos of the property, as well as share updates about open houses and price reductions.
2. **Email marketing** is another effective online marketing strategy. Investors can send email campaigns to potential buyers and real estate agents, highlighting the property's unique features and benefits. Online advertising, such as Google Ads or Facebook Ads, can also be used to reach a broader audience.

Offline marketing efforts can include direct mail, flyers, and open houses.

1. **Direct mail** campaigns can be targeted to *potential buyers* or *real estate agents* in the area. Investors can use direct mail to promote *open houses*, announce *price reductions*, or highlight *unique features* of the property. A well-designed direct mail campaign can grab the recipient's attention and pique their interest in the property. Direct mail can also be highly targeted, making it a cost-effective way to reach potential buyers or real estate agents who have previously shown interest in similar properties.
2. **Flyers** can be distributed in the local community or left at the property during open houses. Flyers should include *high-quality photos* of the property, its unique selling points, and contact information for the investor or their agent. By distributing flyers in *high-traffic areas*, such as local businesses or community centers, investors can increase exposure and generate interest in the property.
3. Finally, **open houses** are an essential part of the marketing process, allowing potential buyers to tour the property and

envision themselves living in it. Investors should prepare the property for open houses by *staging* it and making sure it is clean and inviting. During the open house, investors or their agent should be available to *answer questions* and provide additional information about the property. By creating a welcoming and informative environment, investors can make potential buyers feel more comfortable and increase the chances of a successful sale.

12.3 Staging and Preparing Your Fix and Flip Property for Sale

Staging and preparing a fix and flip property for sale is an important part of the marketing process.

1. Staging involves creating an atmosphere that appeals to potential buyers and **showcases the property's best features**. It can include *furniture placement*, *lighting*, and *decorative accents*. Investors can hire a *professional staging company* to stage the property or do it themselves. If investors choose to do it themselves, they should focus on creating a neutral, inviting atmosphere that appeals to a broad range of potential buyers. This can include *removing personal items*, *decluttering*, and creating a flow throughout the property.
2. Preparing a property for sale involves ensuring that it is **clean, decluttered, and in good repai**r. This can include repairing any visible damage, such as holes in walls or broken tiles, as well as ensuring that all appliances and systems are in working order.
3. Investors should also consider having the **property inspected** to identify any potential issues that may arise during the sale process.
4. Investors should also pay attention to **curb appeal** when

preparing the property for sale. This can include *landscaping*, *cleaning the exterior*, and ensuring that the property has a *welcoming entrance*. Curb appeal is the first impression that potential buyers will have of the property, and it can significantly impact their decision to view the property.

12.4 How to Price and Market Your Properties for Maximum ROI

There are several tactics you can use to price and market your properties for maximum ROI:

1. When determining the sale price of a fix and flip property, investors should **research comparable properties** in the area that have *similar features and amenities*. They should look at recent sales data to determine the average price per square foot for similar properties and make adjustments based on the size and condition of the property they are selling. Investors can also look at properties that are currently on the market to see how they are priced relative to their own property.
2. Another important factor to consider when pricing a fix and flip property is the **quality of the renovation**. A high-quality renovation can justify a *higher price* point and attract buyers who are willing to pay more for a move-in ready home. On the other hand, a subpar renovation may require a *lower price* point to attract buyers who are willing to put in the work to make the home livable.
3. When it comes to marketing the property, investors should **highlight the unique features** and benefits of the property to potential buyers. For example, if the property is located in a *desirable neighborhood* or has a *spacious backyard*, these features should be emphasized in the marketing materials.

Investors can use *high-quality photos* and *virtual tours* to showcase the property and provide potential buyers with a clear picture of what the property looks like and how it feels to be inside.

4. Finally, pricing and marketing strategies should be adjusted based on **market conditions** and feedback from potential buyers. If the market is slow and properties are sitting on the market for an extended period, investors may need to *lower the price* or adjust their marketing strategy to reach a wider audience. Conversely, if there is a lot of demand for properties in the area, investors may be able to *price the property higher* and focus on more targeted marketing efforts to attract the right buyers.

12.5 Leveraging Social Media and Other Online Channels for Property Marketing

Social media and other online channels are essential for marketing fix and flip properties.

1. **Social media** platforms like Facebook, Instagram, and Twitter offer a broad audience and the ability to target specific demographics. Investors should create a social media presence for the property and post high-quality photos and videos regularly. They can also share updates about open houses, price reductions, and any unique features of the property.
2. **Online advertising**, such as Google Ads or Facebook Ads, can also be used to reach a broader audience.
3. **Email marketing** is another effective online marketing strategy. Investors can send email campaigns to potential buyers and real estate agents, highlighting the property's unique features and benefits.

4. Investors should also consider listing the property on **online real estate marketplaces** like Craigslist, Zillow and Realtor.com. These websites offer a broad audience and allow potential buyers to search for properties by location, price, and features.

Online marketing strategies should be adjusted based on market conditions and feedback from potential buyers.

12.6 Finding and Working with Real Estate Agents to Sell Your Fix and Flip Property

Real estate agents can be an essential part of the fix and flip property selling process. They have access to a broad **network of potential buyers** and can provide valuable insights into the *local real estate market*. Investors should carefully select a real estate agent based on their experience, reputation, and knowledge of the local market.

Investors should also have **clear communication** with their real estate agents regarding their goals, timelines, and expectations. Real estate agents can also *handle negotiations* and help to ensure a smooth closing process.

Investors should also consider offering an **additional commission** to the buyer's agent to *incentivize* them to show the property to their clients. This can help to increase the property's exposure and attract potential buyers.

12.7 Closing the Sale and Maximizing Your Returns

Closing the sale of a fix and flip property is an important step towards realizing the maximum return on investment (ROI). It involves the **finalization of the sale** and **transfer of the property's ownership** to the buyer. To ensure a smooth closing process, investors should work closely with their real estate agent and attorney, who can guide them through the necessary steps.

1. The closing process typically involves **reviewing and signing several documents**, such as the *settlement statement*, *title insurance*, and *mortgage documents*. It is essential to carefully review these documents to ensure that all details are accurate and to avoid any potential legal or financial issues.
2. Another critical aspect of closing the sale is ensuring that **all necessary inspections and repairs** have been completed. Investors should have conducted a **final walkthrough** to ensure that the property is in the condition agreed upon with the buyer. Any outstanding repairs should be completed before closing to avoid delays or issues.
3. After the property has been sold, investors should **evaluate their returns** to determine the success of the investment. This can involve calculating the *profit margin*, *ROI*, and other metrics. Evaluating the marketing and selling strategies used can also help identify areas for improvement in future investments.
4. **Reinvesting profits** from a successful fix and flip project can help grow an investor's real estate portfolio and *increase overall returns*. Investors may also consider other investment strategies, such as rental properties or commercial real estate, to *diversify* their portfolio and maximize their long-term returns.

Conclusion

Marketing and selling a fix and flip property is a crucial aspect of the investment process. Investors must understand the importance of marketing and create a comprehensive marketing plan to reach potential buyers. Staging and preparing the property for sale is also essential to attract potential buyers and maximize ROI.

Investors should also carefully price and market the property, leveraging social media and other online channels to reach a broad audience. Working with real estate agents can also provide valuable insights and help to ensure a smooth selling process.

Finally, closing the sale and analyzing returns are critical steps in the fix and flip investment process. By carefully evaluating their marketing and selling strategies and reinvesting their profits, investors can continue to grow their real estate portfolio and increase their overall returns.

Chapter 13: Managing Risk in Fix and Flip Investing

Risky - Photo by Jack Sloop

Fix and flip investing can be a lucrative way to invest in real estate, but it is not without risks. Investors must understand the potential risks and take steps to mitigate them to protect their investments. In this chapter, we will discuss how to identify and manage risks in fix and flip investing.

13.1 Identifying and Mitigating Risks in Fix and Flip Investing

Fix and flip investing involves purchasing a distressed property, renovating it, and then selling it for a profit. While it can be a profitable investment strategy, it also carries risks that can affect the project's success. The following are some steps you can take to handle risks:

1. **Identifying potential risks:** Market risks include fluctuations in *interest rates, supply and demand imbalances,*

and *economic downturns*. Property-specific risks can include unexpected repairs, delays, cost overruns, and issues with contractors or other professionals involved in the project.

2. **Mitigating risks:** To mitigate risks, investors should conduct thorough *due diligence* on the property, market, and professionals they plan to work with. Due diligence includes inspecting the property for potential issues and reviewing its history and the local real estate market conditions. The investor should also carefully select contractors and suppliers with *proven track records* and credentials. In addition, investors should create a *contingency plan* for unexpected events that may occur during the renovation process. This can include setting aside a *reserve fund* for unexpected repairs, delays, and other challenges.
3. **Communication:** Effective communication with stakeholders is essential for mitigating risks. Investors should maintain an open line of communication with *contractors*, *lenders*, and *real estate agents* to ensure that everyone is aware of *potential risks* and how they will be addressed. For example, if unexpected repairs arise, the investor should communicate the issue with the contractor and work together to come up with a plan to resolve it. Open communication can help prevent small issues from turning into bigger problems that can derail the project.

Overall, identifying and mitigating risks in fix and flip investing requires *careful planning*, *due diligence*, and *effective communication* with all stakeholders. By taking these steps, investors can help minimize the impact of potential risks and increase the chances of a successful project.

13.2 Understanding the Different Types of Risks in Real Estate Investing

Real estate investing involves a variety of risks, including market risks, property-specific risks, financing risks, and legal risks.

1. **Market Risks:** To understand market risks, investors must analyze the *local real estate market and economic conditions.* This includes researching trends in *supply and demand, vacancy rates, rental rates*, and *property values*. Investors can also analyze *interest rate trends* and *economic indicators* such as GDP, inflation, and unemployment rates. Understanding market risks can help investors make informed decisions about when and where to invest in real estate.
2. **Property-Specific Risks:** To understand property-specific risks, investors should conduct thorough *due diligence* on the property they plan to invest in. This includes *hiring a home inspector* to *identify potential issues, reviewing the property's history* and any liens or encumbrances, and researching zoning and building codes. Investors can also consult with real estate agents, contractors, and other professionals to help identify potential property-specific risks.
3. **Financing Risks:** To understand financing risks, investors should research the *different types of financing available* and the requirements for each. Investors should also analyze interest rate trends and any potential changes in loan terms that may impact their ability to make payments. Investors can mitigate financing risks by building a strong credit history, maintaining a low debt-to-income ratio, and setting aside reserves for unexpected expenses.
4. **Legal Risks:** To understand legal risks, investors should *consult with attorneys* to understand the legal requirements involved in real estate investing. Investors should also

carefully review contracts and agreements with contractors, tenants, and other stakeholders to ensure that all parties are clear on their responsibilities. Maintaining open communication with stakeholders can also help mitigate legal risks.

In summary, understanding the different types of risks in real estate investing requires research, due diligence, and consultation with professionals. Mitigating these risks involves taking steps to minimize the impact of unexpected challenges and maintaining open communication with stakeholders. By taking these steps, investors can help protect their investments and increase their chances of success in real estate investing.

Investors must understand these different types of risks and take steps to mitigate them to protect their investments.

13.3 Strategies for Minimizing Risk in Fix and Flip Projects

There are several strategies that investors can use to minimize risk in fix and flip projects.

1. **Conducting thorough due diligence:** Before investing in a fix and flip project, it's essential to conduct thorough due diligence on both the *property and the market.* This can involve researching the property's history, including any liens or encumbrances, as well as analyzing the local real estate market and economic conditions. Investors should also consider the *potential demand for the property*, *its location*, and the *potential return on investmen*t.
2. **Careful selection of contractors and suppliers:** Selecting the right contractors and suppliers is crucial to the success of a fix and flip project. Investors should research potential

contractors and suppliers, checking their credentials, references, and past work history. Investors should also ensure that *contractors are licensed and insured* and have experience working on similar projects.

3. **Maintaining open communication:** Open communication is essential in minimizing risk in fix and flip projects. Investors should maintain open lines of communication with contractors, suppliers, lenders, and other stakeholders to ensure that everyone is aware of potential risks and how they will be addressed. Investors should also ensure that they have a *clear understanding of the progress* of the project and any issues that arise.
4. **Having a contingency plan:** Having a contingency plan for unexpected challenges is essential in minimizing risk in fix and flip projects. Investors should set aside a *reserve fund* for *unexpected repairs or delays* and have alternative financing options in place in case of challenges obtaining traditional financing. Having a solid contingency plan can help investors avoid financial setbacks and minimize the impact of unexpected challenges.
5. **Working with experienced professionals:** Investors should consider working with experienced professionals, such as real estate agents and attorneys, to ensure that their investments are properly protected. Real estate agents can help investors identify potential properties, while attorneys can assist with legal issues related to the project. Working with experienced professionals can provide investors with *valuable insights* and help *minimize risk* in fix and flip projects.

In summary, minimizing risk in fix and flip projects requires careful planning, thorough due diligence, and open communication with stakeholders. Investors should also have a contingency plan in place and consider working with experienced professionals to ensure the success of their investments.

13.4 How to Protect Your Investments with Insurance and Legal Agreements

Insurance and legal agreements can also help to protect fix and flip investments.

1. **Property insurance** can provide coverage for *unexpected events* such as fire, theft, or natural disasters. *Liability insurance* can protect investors from legal claims related to injuries or damage that occur on the property. Investors should carefully review their insurance policies to ensure they have adequate coverage for their specific project.
2. **Legal agreements** are important in fix and flip investing to ensure that all parties involved understand their roles and responsibilities. *Contracts with contractors* should outline the scope of work, payment terms, and deadlines. *Contracts with tenants* should outline the *terms of the lease*, including *rent*, *security deposits*, and *maintenance responsibilities*. These agreements should also include provisions for handling disputes or unexpected events.
3. **Forming a legal entity**, such as an LLC, can provide additional protection for investors. By separating personal assets from the investment property, investors can *limit their personal liability* in the event of legal claims related to the property. This can also provide tax benefits and make it easier to obtain financing for future projects. Investors should consult with a lawyer or accountant to determine the best legal structure for their specific situation.

13.5 Dealing with Unexpected Challenges and Risks in

Fix and Flip Investing

Despite careful planning and risk mitigation strategies, unexpected challenges and risks can still arise in fix and flip investing. Investors must be prepared to address these challenges in a timely and effective manner to protect their investments.

1. Having a **contingency plan** in place can be a lifesaver when unexpected challenges arise during the fix and flip process. This plan can include *alternative financing* options or a *reserve fund* set aside for unexpected repairs or delays. Investors should also maintain **open communication** with all stakeholders involved in the project, such as contractors, real estate agents, and lenders. By being proactive and addressing potential risks before they become major issues, investors can minimize the impact of unexpected challenges on their investment.
2. When **unexpected challenges** do arise, investors should act quickly and decisively to address them. This may involve *renegotiating contracts* with contractors to ensure that work is completed on time and within budget, finding *alternative financing* options to cover unexpected expenses, or adjusting the scope or timeline of the project to better align with available resources.
3. In some cases, investors may need to make **difficult decisions** in order to protect their investments. For example, if **unexpected expenses** or delays threaten to consume too much of the project's budget or timeline, investors may need to **consider selling** the property before completing the planned renovations. While this can be a difficult decision, it may be necessary in order to avoid losing money on the investment.

Overall, dealing with unexpected challenges and risks is an inevitable part of fix and flip investing. By being proactive, having a contingency plan in place, and making difficult decisions when necessary, investors can protect their investments and achieve success in this challenging but rewarding market

Conclusion

Fix and flip investing can be a profitable way to invest in real estate, but it is not without risks. Investors must take steps to identify and mitigate potential risks, including conducting thorough due diligence, selecting contractors and suppliers carefully, and having a contingency plan in place for unexpected challenges.

Insurance and legal agreements can also help to protect investments, and investors should be prepared to address unexpected challenges in a timely and effective manner.

By understanding the different types of risks in real estate investing and taking proactive steps to mitigate them, investors can protect their investments and increase their chances of success in fix and flip investing.

Chapter 14: Exit Strategies for Fix and Flip Properties

Exit Strategy - Photo by Keagan Henman

Fix and flip properties can be a great investment opportunity for real estate investors. However, one of the most critical factors for success is having a solid exit strategy in place. An exit strategy is a plan that outlines how an investor intends to sell or dispose of an asset to realize profits. The exit strategy for a fix and flip property can significantly impact the investor's return on investment (ROI). In this chapter, we'll explore different exit strategies for fix and flip properties, including selling, renting, and other strategies. We'll also provide insights into how to plan your exit strategy from the beginning of your fix and flip projects.

14.1 Understanding the Different Exit Strategies for Fix and Flip Properties

There are several exit strategies that investors can employ when fixing and flipping properties.

1. One of the most common strategies is **selling the property** after renovations are completed. This strategy is ideal for investors who want to *realize their profits quickly* and move on to other projects. Selling the property immediately after completing renovations can provide investors with a lump sum of cash, which they can use to finance other investments.
2. The other common exit strategy is **renting the property for long-term cash flow**. This strategy is ideal for investors who want to generate *ongoing income* from their properties. Renting the property can provide investors with a steady stream of cash flow, which they can use to finance *other investments* or supplement their income. It's important to note that this strategy requires investors to have a *long-term mindset* since they won't realize profits until they sell the property.

14.2 Selling Your Properties for Maximum ROI

Selling a fix and flip property can be an excellent exit strategy for investors who want to realize profits quickly. However, to sell the property for maximum ROI, investors need to consider several factors.

1. One of the most critical factors is **pricing the property correctly**. Pricing the property too high can deter potential buyers, while pricing it too low can result in missed opportunities for profits. Investors need to do their due diligence and research the local market to determine the optimal price for the property.
2. Another critical factor to consider when selling a fix and flip property is **staging the property**. Staging involves arranging furniture and decor in a way that showcases the property's features and makes it attractive to potential buyers. Staging can help buyers envision themselves living in the property,

which can increase their willingness to make an offer.

3. Investors also need to consider **marketing** when selling their fix and flip properties. Marketing involves creating a comprehensive marketing plan that includes listing the property on multiple online platforms, such as real estate websites and social media. The marketing plan should also include high-quality photos and videos that showcase the property's features.

14.3 Renting Your Properties for Long-Term Cash Flow

Renting a fix and flip property can be an excellent exit strategy for investors who want to generate ongoing income from their properties. However, to rent the property for long-term cash flow, investors need to consider several factors.

1. One of the most critical factors is **screening potential tenants**. Screening potential tenants involves checking their credit score, employment history, and rental history to ensure they are financially stable and responsible.
2. Another critical factor to consider when renting a fix and flip property is **managing the property** effectively. Managing the property involves ensuring that the property is well-maintained and that any issues or repairs are addressed promptly. It also involves collecting rent and addressing any tenant concerns or complaints. Investors can manage the property themselves or hire a property management company to handle these tasks for them.
3. Investors also need to consider the **local rental market** when renting their fix and flip properties. They should research the rental rates in the area and set the rent for their property accordingly. Setting the rent too high can deter potential tenants, while setting it too low can result in missed

opportunities for profits.

4. Finally, investors should also consider the **tax implications** of renting their fix and flip properties. They should consult with a tax professional to understand the tax implications of rental income, property depreciation, and other expenses.

14.4 Strategies for Exiting Your Investments at the Right Time

Timing is critical when it comes to exiting fix and flip investments. Investors need to consider market conditions and economic factors to determine the best time to exit their investments.

1. One strategy for exiting at the right time is to have a **clear exit strategy** from the beginning of the project. Investors should determine their desired exit strategy before they even purchase the property, and they should develop a plan to execute that strategy.
2. Another strategy for exiting at the right time is to **monitor market conditions** and **economic factors** closely. Investors should keep an eye on *interest rates*, *housing inventory*, and *local economic indicators* to determine the best time to sell or rent their properties. They should also have a backup plan in case market conditions change unexpectedly.
3. If an investor has retained some properties they can also employ a strategy called "**scaling out**" to exit their investments at the right time. Scaling out involves **selling some of the properties** in an investor's portfolio to *realize profits* and *reduce risk*. This strategy can be useful when market conditions are uncertain, and investors want to reduce their exposure to risk.

14.5 How to Plan Your Exit Strategy from the Beginning

of Your Fix and Flip Projects

Planning your exit strategy from the beginning of your fix and flip projects can help you maximize your ROI and minimize your risk.

1. One of the first steps in planning your exit strategy is to **determine your investment goals**. Do you want to realize profits quickly, generate ongoing cash flow, or a combination of both? Once you've determined your investment goals, you can develop a plan to achieve them.
2. Another important step in planning your exit strategy is to **research the local real estate market**. You should research *housing inventory*, *rental rates*, and *recent sales data* to determine the optimal time to sell or rent your property. You should also consider any economic factors or market trends that may impact your investment.
3. Investors should also **develop a budget and timeline** for their fix and flip projects. This budget and timeline should include all of the expenses associated with the project, including *acquisition costs*, *renovation costs*, and *holding costs*. It should also include a realistic timeline for completing the project and executing your exit strategy.
4. Finally, investors should consider any potential risks or challenges associated with their fix and flip projects. They should have a **backup plan** in case of unexpected issues, such as unexpected repair costs or difficulty finding tenants or buyers.

Conclusion

Having a solid exit strategy is critical for success when investing in fix and flip properties. Investors can employ several exit strategies, including selling, renting, lease-option agreements, seller financing, and refinancing. To maximize ROI and minimize risk, investors should plan their exit strategy from the beginning of their fix and flip projects. They should determine their investment goals, research the local real estate market, develop a budget and timeline, and consider potential risks and challenges. By doing so, investors can increase their chances of success and achieve their investment goals.

Chapter 15: Understanding Real Estate Laws and Regulations

Laws - Photo by Aleix Ventayol

Real estate investing can be a profitable venture, but it comes with many legal and regulatory requirements that investors must comply with. Understanding real estate laws and regulations is essential for investors to avoid legal issues and liability risks. This chapter will provide an overview of the basics of real estate law and regulation, zoning, building codes, permitting, managing legal and liability risks in fix and flip projects, compliance with fair housing laws and other regulations, and navigating tax laws and regulations in real estate investing.

15.1 Basics of Real Estate Law and Regulation

Real estate law and regulations govern the buying, selling, leasing, and financing of real estate properties.

Investors must comply with **state and federal laws** related to real estate transactions, such as contract law, property law, and tort law.

1. **Contract law** governs the creation and enforcement of real estate contracts,
2. **Property law** governs the ownership and use of real estate properties.
3. **Tort law** governs civil wrongs, such as negligence, that may result in injury or damage to a person or property.

Investors must also comply with various **regulations related to real estate transactions**, such as environmental regulations, building codes, and zoning laws. *Environmental regulations* govern the impact of real estate projects on the environment, while *building codes* and *zoning laws* govern the construction and use of real estate properties. Failure to comply with these regulations can result in legal issues and liability risks.

15.2 Understanding Zoning, Building Codes, and Permitting

Zoning laws and building codes are critical aspects of real estate regulation that investors must understand.

1. **Zoning laws** regulate the use of land within a municipality, such as residential, commercial, or industrial use. Investors must comply with zoning laws when choosing a location for their real estate projects.
2. **Building codes** regulate the construction and safety standards for buildings, and investors must comply with building codes when renovating or constructing real estate properties.
3. **Permitting** is another critical aspect of real estate regulation

that investors must understand. Permits are required for many real estate projects, such as construction, renovation, and demolition. Investors must obtain the necessary permits before beginning their projects to avoid legal issues and liability risks.

15.3 Managing Legal and Liability Risks in Fix and Flip Projects

Fix and flip projects come with many legal and liability risks that investors must manage.

1. One of the most significant risks is the risk of **personal injury** or **property damage** during the renovation process. Investors must ensure that their projects comply with building codes and safety standards to avoid these risks. They should also obtain *insurance coverage* to protect themselves against liability claims.
2. Investors must also ensure that they have **clear title** to the property before beginning their fix and flip projects. Title issues, such as *liens or easements*, can result in legal issues and delays in the project. Investors should conduct a title search to ensure that they have clear title to the property.
3. Another critical aspect of managing legal and liability risks in fix and flip projects is to comply with **fair housing laws**. Fair housing laws prohibit discrimination based on race, color, national origin, religion, sex, familial status, or disability. Investors must ensure that they comply with these laws when renting or selling their properties to avoid legal issues.

15.4 Compliance with Fair Housing Laws and Other Regulations

Compliance with fair housing laws and other regulations is critical for real estate investors to avoid legal issues and liability risks.

1. **Fair housing laws** prohibit discrimination based on certain protected classes, and investors must ensure that they comply with these laws when renting or selling their properties.
2. They should also ensure that their properties comply with the **Americans with Disabilities Act (ADA)**, which requires that buildings be accessible to individuals with disabilities.
3. Investors must also comply with **environmental regulations**, such as the Clean Air Act, the Clean Water Act, and the Resource Conservation and Recovery Act. These regulations govern the impact of real estate projects on the environment and require investors to take measures to reduce their environmental impact.
4. **Tax laws and regulations** are another critical aspect of real estate investing that investors must navigate. Real estate investments are subject to various taxes, such as property taxes, capital gains taxes, and income taxes. Investors must understand these taxes and ensure that they comply with applicable tax laws and regulations to avoid legal issues and penalties.

15.5 Navigating Tax Laws and Regulations in Real Estate Investing

Navigating tax laws and regulations is a critical aspect of real estate investing. Investors must understand the various taxes that apply to real estate investments, such as property taxes, capital gains taxes, and income taxes.

1. **Property taxes** are taxes that are assessed on the value of real estate properties and are paid annually.
2. **Capital gains taxes** are taxes that are assessed on the profit that is earned from the sale of a property.
3. **Income taxes** are taxes that are assessed on the income that is earned from a real estate investment.

Investors must also understand the tax implications of different **real estate investment structures**, such as *partnerships*, *LLCs*, and *corporations*. Each investment structure has different tax implications, and investors must choose the structure that is most advantageous for their investment goals. Investors should seek advice from professionals.

Another critical aspect of navigating tax laws and regulations in real estate investing is to understand the various **tax deductions and credits** that are available. Real estate investors can take advantage of various tax deductions and credits, such as depreciation deductions, mortgage interest deductions, and energy tax credits. Investors must understand these deductions and credits and ensure that they take advantage of them to reduce their tax liability.

Conclusion

Real estate laws and regulations are complex and can be challenging for investors to navigate. Understanding these laws and regulations is essential for investors to avoid legal issues and liability risks. Investors must understand the basics of real estate law and regulation, zoning, building codes, and permitting, managing legal and liability risks in fix and flip projects, compliance with fair housing laws and other regulations, and navigating tax laws and regulations in real estate investing. By understanding these aspects of real estate regulation, investors can ensure that they comply with applicable laws and regulations and avoid legal issues and liability risks.

Chapter 16: Scaling Your Fix and Flip Real Estate Investing Business

Scaling - Photo by The Lazy Artist Gallery

Fix and flip real estate investing can be a lucrative business, but it requires more than just finding the right property and flipping it for a profit. To truly succeed in this industry, you need a long-term strategy for scaling your business and staying competitive in the market. This chapter will explore various ways to scale your fix and flip investing business, including expanding into other real estate investing strategies and building a strong team.

16.1 Developing a Long-Term Fix and Flip Investing Strategy

To scale your fix and flip investing business, you need a long-term strategy that outlines your goals, timelines, and resources.

1. Start by assessing your current business and identifying **areas for improvement**. Consider your strengths and weaknesses

and determine how you can leverage your strengths to expand your business.

2. Next, set **specific goals and timelines** for your business. Determine how many properties you want to flip each year and how much revenue you want to generate. Identify the resources you need to achieve these goals, such as funding, marketing, and staffing.
3. Finally, develop a **marketing plan to promote your business** and attract new clients. This may include building a website, networking with other real estate professionals, and advertising through social media and other channels.

16.2 How to Grow Your Fix and Flip Business

There are several strategies for growing your fix and flip business, including increasing your marketing efforts, expanding your geographic reach, and partnering with other investors or real estate professionals.

1. One effective way to grow your business is to **increase your marketing efforts**. This may include advertising through *social media*, *email marketing*, *direct mail campaigns*, and targeted online advertising. You can also attend networking events and industry conferences to meet potential clients and build relationships with other real estate professionals.
2. Another way to scale your business is to **expand your geographic reach**. Consider investing in properties in different regions or expanding your services to other cities or states. This can help diversify your portfolio and reduce your risk.
3. Finally, **partnering with other investors** or real estate professionals can help you grow your business by providing access to new resources and expertise. You can partner with

other fix and flip investors, real estate agents, or lenders to share knowledge, funding, and contacts.

16.3 Expanding into Other Real Estate Investing Strategies

To further scale your business, consider expanding into other real estate investing strategies, such as rental properties, commercial real estate, or real estate development. By diversifying your portfolio, you can reduce your risk and increase your potential for long-term growth and profitability.

1. **Rental properties** can provide a stable source of income and long-term appreciation potential. You can invest in *single-family homes*, *multi-unit properties*, or *commercial properties*, depending on your goals and resources.
2. **Commercial real estate** can provide higher returns but also requires more expertise and resources. You can invest in *office buildings*, *retail centers*, or *industrial properties*, among others.
3. **Real estate development** involves building new properties or renovating existing ones to sell or rent. This can be a more complex and time-consuming strategy but can also offer higher returns.

16.4 Building Your Team and Outsourcing Tasks for Greater Efficiency

As your business grows, you may need to build a team to handle various tasks, such as property management, construction, and marketing. Consider outsourcing tasks to third-party providers, such as property managers, contractors, and marketing agencies, to increase efficiency and reduce your workload.

When building your team, consider the **expertise and experience** of each member and how they can contribute to your overall goals.

You may need to hire:

1. a *project manager* to oversee your fix and flip projects,
2. *a marketing specialist* to promote your business, and
3. a *financial advisor* to manage your investments.

Outsourcing tasks can help you *focus on your core strengths* and *increase your productivity*. You can outsource tasks such as property management, construction, and marketing to third-party providers who *specialize* in these areas. This can save you time and money while ensuring that each task is completed to a high standard.

When outsourcing tasks, be sure to **research and vet potential providers** to ensure that they are reputable and reliable. You may also want to consider working with providers who specialize in real estate investing, as they will have a better understanding of your specific needs and goals.

16.5 Staying Competitive and Innovating in the Fix and Flip Market

To stay competitive in the fix and flip market, you need to continually innovate and adapt to changing market conditions. This may include investing in new technologies, exploring new marketing channels, or partnering with other investors or real estate professionals.

1. One way to innovate in the fix and flip market is to invest in **new technologies**. For example, you can use *virtual reality technology* to create immersive property tours, or you can use *drones* to capture aerial footage of properties.
2. Another way to stay competitive is to explore **additional**

marketing channels, such as *social media* and *online advertising* that you aren't already using. You can also leverage the power of *content marketing* to establish yourself as an authority in the industry and attract new clients.
3. **Partnering** with other investors or real estate professionals can also help you stay competitive by providing access to new resources and expertise. You can partner with other fix and flip investors, real estate agents, or lenders to share knowledge, funding, and contacts.

Conclusion

Scaling your fix and flip real estate investing business requires a long-term strategy, dedication, and hard work. By developing a clear plan, expanding your services, building a strong team, and staying competitive in the market, you can achieve your goals and build a successful business.

With the right strategy and support, you can achieve long-term success in the fix and flip real estate investing industry.

Chapter 17: Building a Brand and Reputation in Fix and Flip Investing

Brand - Photo by Patrik Michalicka

Building a strong brand and reputation is essential for success in any industry, and fix and flip investing is no exception. Your brand and reputation can influence how clients and partners perceive your business, as well as your ability to attract new business and opportunities.

In this chapter, we will explore the importance of branding and reputation in fix and flip investing, and provide strategies for developing and maintaining a positive brand and reputation in the real estate industry.

17.1 Understanding the Importance of Branding and Reputation in Real Estate Investing

Your brand and reputation are key factors in establishing yourself as a trusted and credible real estate investor.

A **strong brand** can help you *stand out from competitors*. In the fix and flip industry, branding can include everything from your *business name* and *logo*, to your *website* and *social media presence*. Your brand should reflect your *values, mission, and unique selling points*, and should be designed to appeal to your target audience.

A **positive reputation** can help you *attract new clients, investors, and partners*. Your reputation is built on your *track record*, your *professionalism*, and your *ability to deliver* results. A positive reputation can help you *establish trust* and *credibility* with clients, investors, and partners, while a **negative reputation** can *hinder your ability to grow* your business.

17.2 How to Develop Your Brand and Reputation as a Fix and Flip Investor

Developing a strong brand and reputation as a fix and flip investor requires a strategic approach. Here are some strategies to consider:

- Develop a **clear mission statement** and value proposition that reflects your unique selling points.
- Create a **professional website** and **social media presence** that showcases your brand and highlights your experience and expertise.
- Build **relationships** with industry professionals, including *real estate agents*, *lenders*, *contractors*, and *other investors*.
- Establish yourself as an **authority in the industry** by *writing blog posts*, *creating videos*, or *speaking at industry events*.
- Deliver **high-quality results** for your clients, investors, and partners, and strive to exceed expectations.

By following these strategies, you can establish a strong brand and reputation that sets you apart from competitors and attracts new business and opportunities.

17.3 Strategies for Building Trust and Credibility with Your Clients and Partners

Building **trust and credibility** with your clients and partners is essential for success in the fix and flip industry. Here are some strategies to consider:

- **Communicate clearly and consistently** with your clients and partners, keeping them informed about the progress of projects and any challenges that arise.
- **Build strong relationships** with your contractors, ensuring that they deliver high-quality work and meet deadlines.
- **Be transparent and honest** in your dealings with clients, investors, and partners, and always act with integrity.
- **Deliver on your promises** and strive to exceed expectations, building a reputation for reliability and excellence.
- **Address any issues or complaints** promptly and professionally, working to resolve them in a way that satisfies all parties involved.

By building trust and credibility with your clients and partners, you can establish yourself as a trusted and respected fix and flip investor, and build a positive reputation in the industry.

17.4 Best Practices for Maintaining a Positive Reputation in the Real Estate Industry

Maintaining a **positive reputation** in the real estate industry requires ongoing effort and attention. Here are some best practices to consider:

- **Act professionally and ethically** in all your dealings with clients, investors, and partners: To maintain a positive reputation in the real estate industry, it is essential to act professionally and ethically at all times. This means being *honest, transparent, and trustworthy* in all dealings with clients, investors, and partners. It is crucial to always put their interests first and provide them with accurate and relevant information to make informed decisions. Avoid using any *unethical or illegal practices* that could damage your reputation and result in legal consequences.
- **Respond promptly and professionally** to inquiries and requests for information: In the real estate industry, time is of the essence. Promptly responding to inquiries and requests for information can help establish trust and credibility with potential clients and investors. Ensure that you are *reachable through multiple channels* and respond in a professional and courteous manner. Always be prepared to answer questions, provide information, and offer solutions that can help build and maintain positive relationships.
- **Deliver high-quality results** and strive to exceed expectations: Providing high-quality results is essential for maintaining a positive reputation in the real estate industry. Strive to deliver top-notch services that meet or exceed the expectations of clients and investors. This can include being *detail-oriented*, using *high-quality materials*, and *working with skilled professionals*.
- **Take responsibility for any mistakes or issues** that arise, and work to resolve them in a timely and effective manner: Mistakes and issues can happen in any business, including real estate. However, it's how you handle them that can make a significant impact on your reputation. If an issue arises, take

responsibility and *work to resolve it promptly and effectively.* This can involve being *proactive in addressing the issue*, *offering solutions*, and *keeping all stakeholders informed* of the progress.

- **Build a strong network of industry professionals** and maintain positive relationships with them: Building a strong network of industry professionals is crucial for success in the real estate industry. This can include real estate agents, contractors, appraisers, inspectors, and other professionals. *Networking* can help you establish valuable connections and access important resources that can help you grow your business. *Maintaining positive relationships* with industry professionals can also help build credibility and establish a positive reputation in the industry. Attend industry events, participate in professional organizations, and engage with other professionals to build and maintain your network.

By following these best practices, you can maintain a positive reputation in the real estate industry and establish yourself as a trusted and respected fix and flip investor.

17.5 How to Leverage Your Brand and Reputation for Greater Success in Fix and Flip Investing

Your brand and reputation can be powerful assets in the fix and flip industry, helping you attract new clients, investors, and partners, and differentiate yourself from competitors. Here are some strategies for leveraging your brand and reputation:

- Use your brand to **establish yourself as an expert** in the industry, creating content and speaking at events to build your profile.
- Use your reputation to **attract new clients and investors**,

highlighting your track record and results.

- **Build a strong referral network** by maintaining positive relationships with past clients, contractors, and industry professionals.
- **Seek out partnerships** with other real estate professionals, leveraging their networks and expertise to grow your business.

By leveraging your brand and reputation, you can position yourself for greater success in the fix and flip industry, and build a sustainable and profitable business.

Conclusion

Building a strong brand and reputation is essential for success in the fix and flip industry. By developing a clear mission statement, creating a professional website and social media presence, and building strong relationships with industry professionals, you can establish yourself as a trusted and respected fix and flip investor.

To maintain a positive reputation, it's important to act professionally and ethically in all your dealings, deliver high-quality results, and build strong relationships with clients, investors, and partners. By leveraging your brand and reputation, you can attract new business and opportunities, and position yourself for greater success in the fix and flip industry.

Chapter 18: The Future of Fix and Flip Investing

Future - Photo by Tomasz Frankowski

Fix and flip investing is a popular real estate investment strategy where an investor buys a distressed property, renovates it, and then sells it for a profit. This strategy has gained popularity over the years due to the potential for high returns on investment. However, as with any investment, the fix and flip industry is not immune to market changes, trends, and innovations. In this chapter, we will explore the future of fix and flip investing, including trends, predictions, emerging technologies, and challenges. We will also discuss how investors can stay ahead of the curve and thrive in the evolving fix and flip real estate industry.

18.1 Trends and Predictions for the Fix and Flip Real Estate Market

The fix and flip market has experienced significant growth over the years, and this trend is expected to continue in the future.

1. One trend that is likely to shape the future of fix and flip investing is the **shift towards urban areas**. In recent years, there has been a growing demand for properties in urban areas due to factors such as *proximity to job opportunities and amenities*. This trend is expected to continue in the future, with more investors focusing on acquiring properties in urban areas.
2. Another trend that is likely to shape the future of fix and flip investing is the **growing interest in sustainable and eco-friendly homes**. With the increasing awareness of *environmental issues*, more investors are looking for ways to make their properties eco-friendly, such as installing solar panels, energy-efficient windows, and appliances.

18.2 Emerging Technologies and Innovations in Fix and Flip Investing

The use of technology has revolutionized many industries, including real estate, and fix and flip investing is no exception.

1. One of the emerging technologies that is likely to shape the future of fix and flip investing is **virtual reality (VR)**. VR technology allows investors to tour a property virtually, saving time and resources that would otherwise be spent physically visiting the property. This technology can also be used to stage properties virtually, making it easier for investors to showcase a property's potential to potential buyers.
2. Another emerging technology in fix and flip investing is **blockchain**. Blockchain technology can be used to streamline the property buying and selling process, making it more transparent and efficient. By using blockchain technology, investors can also ensure that their transactions

are secure, minimizing the risk of fraud.

18.3 Opportunities and Challenges in the Future of Fix and Flip Investing

As with any investment, there are both opportunities and challenges in the fix and flip industry.

1. One of the **opportunities** in the future of fix and flip investing is the **growing demand for housing**. According to a report by the National Association of Realtors, the U.S. is facing a housing shortage, with demand outstripping supply. This presents an opportunity for fix and flip investors to acquire distressed properties, renovate them, and sell them at a profit.
2. One of the **challenges** in the future of fix and flip investing is the **competition**. With the increasing popularity of fix and flip investing, the market is becoming more crowded, making it more challenging to find good investment opportunities. This means that investors will need to be *more creative in finding investment opportunities* and have a thorough understanding of the market to succeed.

18.4 How to Stay Ahead of the Curve in the Evolving Fix and Flip Real Estate Industry

To stay ahead of the curve in the evolving fix and flip real estate industry:

1. investors need to stay up to date with **industry trends and innovations**. This means attending industry events, reading industry publications, and networking with other industry professionals.
2. Additionally, investors need to be *flexible and adaptable* to

changes in the market. This means being willing to *pivot their investment strategy* if necessary and being *open to new technologies* and innovations.

3. Another way to stay ahead of the curve in the fix and flip industry is to **work with experienced professionals**. This includes working with a *reputable real estate agent*, *contractor*, and other professionals who can provide valuable insights and guidance throughout the investment process.
4. Additionally, investors should consider **partnering** with other investors to share resources and knowledge.

18.5 Strategies for Thriving in the Future of Fix and Flip Investing

1. To thrive in the future of fix and flip investing, investors need to have a **solid investment strategy.** This includes identifying profitable *investment opportunities*, conducting thorough *due diligence*, and accurately assessing the *cost of renovations*.
2. Additionally, investors should have a **well-defined marketing strategy** to attract potential buyers and maximize their returns on investment.
3. Another strategy for thriving in the fix and flip industry is to focus on **building a strong reputation**. This includes delivering quality renovations, being transparent with buyers, and maintaining a good relationship with industry professionals. By building a strong reputation, investors can attract more investment opportunities and increase their chances of success in the industry.

Conclusion

The future of fix and flip investing is bright, with growing demand for housing and emerging technologies and innovations that can streamline the investment process. However, investors must also be aware of the challenges that come with investing in the fix and flip industry, including competition and market changes. To thrive in this industry, investors must stay ahead of the curve, be flexible and adaptable, and have a solid investment strategy. By following these strategies, investors can capitalize on investment opportunities and achieve success in the fix and flip industry.

Chapter 19: Resources for Fix and Flip Investors

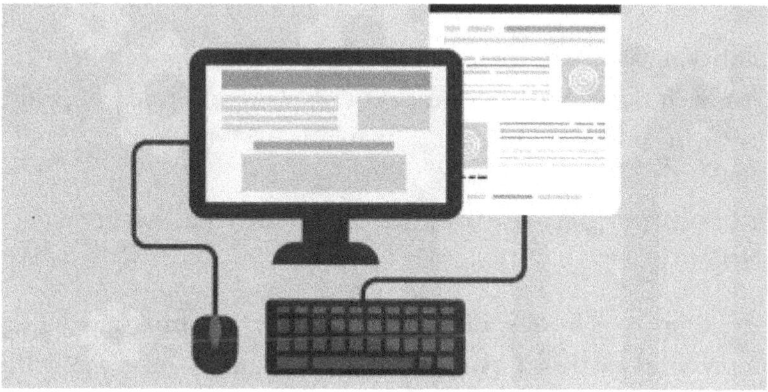

Website - Photo by kreatikar

Fix and flip investing is a profitable business that requires a lot of resources to succeed. Whether you are an experienced investor or a newbie, it is essential to have the right tools and resources at your disposal to make informed decisions and maximize your profits. This chapter provides a comprehensive overview of some of the best resources for fix and flip investors, including tools, websites, apps, recommended books and blogs, professional associations and networks, educational programs and courses, and tips on how to continue your learning and professional development as a fix and flip investor.

19.1 Tools, Websites, and Apps for Fix and Flip Investors

As a fix and flip investor, you need to have access to various tools, websites, and apps to help you make informed decisions and streamline your business operations. Some of the must-have tools for fix and flip investors include **project management software** like ClickUp and Team Gantt, **real estate analysis tools** like Propstream and Property Radar, and **financial management software** like Quicken.

Websites like **BiggerPockets** are also helpful for finding investment opportunities and networking with other investors.

Overall, having access to these tools, websites, and apps can help you stay organized, save time and money, and make informed decisions when investing in real estate.

19.2 Recommended Books and Blogs for Real Estate Investing

There are numerous **books,** including this book, and **blogs**, including jimpellerin.com[1] on real estate investing, specifically on fix and flip invesing.

In terms of blogs, BiggerPockets is a go-to resource for real estate investors, offering a wealth of information on everything from finding deals to financing and managing properties. Other valuable blogs include REtipster, Coach Carson, and Invest Four More.

Overall, reading books and blogs on real estate investing can help you gain valuable knowledge, insights, and ideas that can help you succeed in the fix and flip business.

19.3 Professional Associations and Networks for Real Estate Investors

Professional associations and networks can provide valuable opportunities for fix and flip investors to connect with other investors, learn from industry experts, and stay updated on industry trends and

1. http://jimpellerin.com

developments. The best **professional associations** for real estate investors is the National Real Estate Investors Association (NREIA).

Networking platforms like **Meetup** and **LinkedIn** are also excellent resources for finding and connecting with other investors in your area. Additionally, **attending real estate conferences** and events can provide valuable opportunities to learn from industry experts, network with other investors, and stay updated on the latest trends and developments.

Overall, joining professional associations and networks can help you stay connected with other investors and industry experts, gain valuable insights and ideas, and enhance your success in the fix and flip business.

19.4 Educational Programs and Courses for Fix and Flip Investing

Educational programs and courses can provide valuable insights and training on various aspects of real estate investing, including finding deals, financing, property management, and marketing. Some of the best educational programs and courses for fix and flip investors include those offered by the National Real Estate Investors Association (NREIA), Udemy, Coursera, and LinkedIn Learning. Additionally, some universities offer real estate investing courses and degree programs that can provide a more formal education on the subject.

Overall, investing in educational programs and courses can help you enhance your knowledge and skills in real estate investing, stay updated on the latest trends and developments, and gain a competitive edge in the fix and flip business.

19.5 How to Continue Your Learning and Professional Development as a Fix and Flip Investor

Continuing your learning and professional development is crucial for success in the fix and flip business. Some of the best ways to continue your learning and professional development as a fix and flip investor include:

1. **Reading books and blogs** on real estate investing regularly.
2. Attending **real estate conferences**, **seminars**, and **workshops** to learn from industry experts and network with other investors.
3. **Joining professional associations** and networks to stay updated on industry trends and developments.
4. Investing in **educational programs** and courses to enhance your knowledge and skills.
5. **Seeking mentorship** or coaching from experienced investors in your field.

Overall, investing in your learning and professional development can help you stay ahead of the competition, make informed decisions, and maximize your profits in the fix and flip business.

Conclusion

In conclusion, having access to the right tools, resources, and education is crucial for success in the fix and flip business. Whether you are an experienced investor or a newbie, there are numerous tools, websites, apps, books, blogs, professional associations, and educational programs available to help you enhance your knowledge and skills, stay updated on industry trends, and make informed decisions. By investing in your learning and professional development, you can gain a competitive edge, maximize your profits, and succeed in the fix and flip business.

Chapter 20: Conclusion and Next Steps in Fix and Flip Investing

Finish - Photo by PixLoger

Fix and flip investing has become a popular investment strategy for individuals looking to make a profit in the real estate market. The concept involves purchasing a property, making necessary renovations, and selling it for a profit. As with any investment, there are risks and rewards associated with fix and flip investing. In this chapter, we will recap the strategies and best practices for fix and flip investing, provide tips for success, discuss ways to continue learning and improving skills, and offer final thoughts on the future of fix and flip investing. We will conclude with action steps for individuals looking to get started in fix and flip real estate investing.

20.1 Recap of Fix and Flip Real Estate Investing Strategies and Best Practices

In order to be successful in fix and flip investing, it is important to have a clear strategy and to follow best practices.

1. One important strategy is to have a solid understanding of the **local real estate market**. This involves researching the area where the property is located, understanding the demand for properties in that area, and having a good idea of what properties are selling for in that market.
2. Another key strategy is to have a **clear plan** for the renovation process. This involves having a thorough understanding of the necessary renovations and their associated costs, as well as having a team of reliable contractors to complete the work. Additionally, it is important to have a plan for marketing and selling the property once the renovations are complete.
3. Best practices for fix and flip investing include conducting a thorough **inspection** of the property before purchasing, being mindful of the budget throughout the renovation process, and maintaining a good relationship with contractors and other professionals involved in the project.

20.2 Tips for Success as a Fix and Flip Investor

In addition to following the strategies and best practices outlined above, there are several tips for success as a fix and flip investor.

1. One tip is to have a **backup plan** in case the property does not sell as quickly as anticipated. This may involve renting the property out until the market improves, or even holding onto the property for a longer period of time.
2. Another tip is to be flexible and open to **making changes** to the original renovation plan if necessary. Unexpected issues may arise during the renovation process, and it is important to be able to adapt and make changes as needed.
3. **Networking and building relationships** with other real estate professionals can also be beneficial for fix and flip

investors. This includes real estate agents, lenders, and other investors who may be able to provide valuable insights and advice.

20.3 How to Continue Learning and Improving Your Skills as a Real Estate Investor

The real estate market is constantly evolving, and it is important for fix and flip investors to continue learning and improving their skills.

1. One way to do this is to attend real estate **investment conferences and workshops**, where investors can learn from industry experts and network with other investors.
2. **Reading books and articles** on real estate investing can also be helpful, as can taking online courses and seminars. Staying up-to-date on market trends and changes in real estate laws and regulations is also important for staying ahead in the industry.
3. **Networking** with other real estate professionals and building relationships with mentors can also be a valuable source of learning and growth for fix and flip investors.

20.4 Final Thoughts on the Future of Fix and Flip Investing

Fix and flip investing is a viable investment strategy, but it is important to be mindful of the **risks and rewards** associated with this approach. As the real estate market continues to evolve, fix and flip **investors may need to adapt** and change their strategies in order to stay competitive.

However, with the right knowledge, skills, and approach, fix and flip investing can continue to be a profitable investment strategy for many years to come.

20.5 Action Steps for Getting Started in Fix and Flip Real Estate Investing

For individuals looking to get started in fix and flip real estate investing, there are several action steps to take.

1. The first step is to **research** the local real estate market and identify potential properties that may be suitable for fix and flip investing. This involves analyzing property values, rental rates, and other factors that may impact the success of the investment.
2. Next, it is important to **secure financing** for the project. This may involve obtaining a loan from a bank or other lender, or working with private investors or partners.
3. Once financing is in place, it is important to conduct a thorough **inspection** of the property to identify any potential issues or challenges that may arise during the renovation process. This includes assessing the condition of the property, identifying necessary repairs and upgrades, and estimating the cost of the renovation.
4. After the inspection is complete, it is time to begin the **renovation** process. This involves working with contractors to complete the necessary repairs and upgrades, while staying within the established budget and timeline.
5. Once the renovation is complete, it is time to **market** and **sell** the property. This involves working with a real estate agent or marketing the property on your own, and being mindful of the local real estate market and pricing the property accordingly.

Appendix A: The Step-by-Step Guide to Fix and Flip Real Estate Investing

The Ultimate Fix and Flip Real Estate Investing Strategy is a unique Strategy that helps real estate investors complete more fix and flip deals without having to spend a lot of time looking for properties, renovating the properties, or marketing to sell the properties. The following is a step-by-step guide to fix and flip real estate investing and are the recommended steps you should follow:

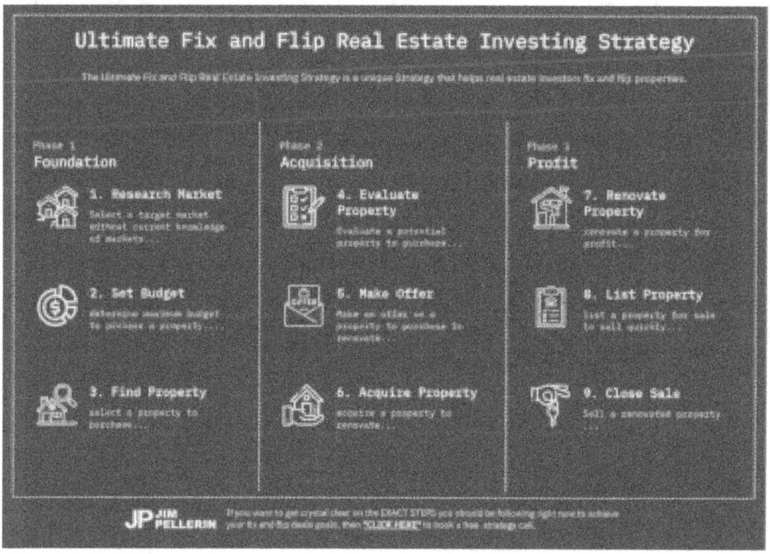

Foundation

1. **Research Market:** Research various markets to locate an area where you are likely to find the best properties that provide the best returns for you.
2. **Set Budget:** Flipping a property requires a significant

amount of capital, so it's important to set a budget before you start looking for properties.

3. **Find Property:** Identify potential properties that fit your criteria. Assess the property's condition and potential for flipping. Consider financing options and calculate the renovation costs.

Acquisition

1. **Evaluate Property:** Next, you will inspect the property for any structural issues, water damage, or other costly repairs that may need to be made. You should also take note of any cosmetic changes that need to be made, such as updating the kitchen or bathrooms.
2. **Make Offer:** Once you've evaluated the property and determined that it's a good investment, it's time to make an offer. Be sure to take into account any repairs or renovations that need to be made when determining your offer price..
3. **Acquire Property:** Once you've made an offer and the purchase and sale agreement is accepted, the next step is to secure financing and acquire the property.

Profit

1. **Renovate Property:** Now, it's time to renovate. Work with contractors and designers to create a renovation plan that will increase the value of the property.
2. **List Property:** Once the renovations are complete, it's time to list it for sale. work with a real estate agent to market the property and find a buyer.
3. **Close Sale:** Once you've found a buyer, it's time to close the sale. This means finalizing all the paperwork and transferring ownership of the property to the new owner.

Foundation

1. Research Market

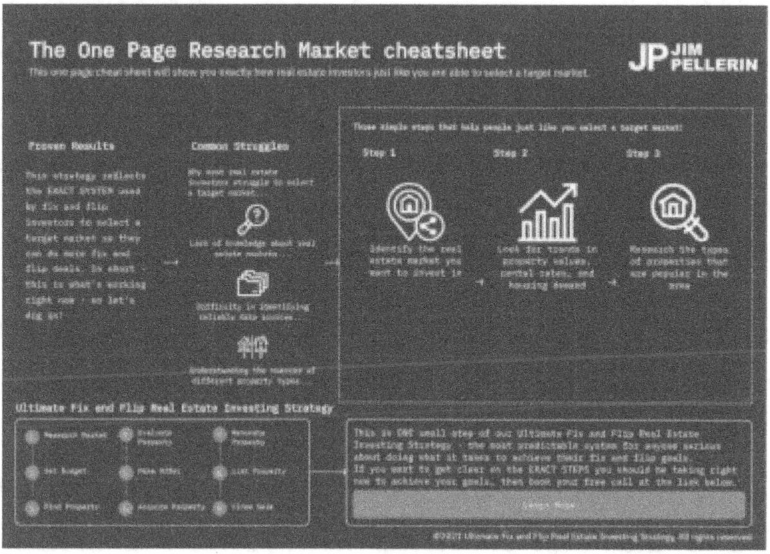

Before you invest in any real estate property, it's important to do your research. This means taking a deep dive into the real estate market in the area where you want to invest. Look for trends in property values, rental rates, and housing demand. You should also research the types of properties that are popular in the area, such as single-family homes, condos, or multi-unit buildings. This research will help you identify the types of properties that are likely to provide the best returns.

Steps

1. Identify the real estate market you want to invest in: Begin by researching and narrowing down your focus to a particular area.

Consider factors such as *location*, *employment opportunities*, *population growth*, and *real estate market trends.*

2. Look for trends in property values, rental rates, and housing demand: Use reliable sources such as *online listing sites*, *real estate agents*, or *local classified sites* to obtain data on property values, rental rates, and housing demand. Look for patterns and trends in the data to help you make informed decisions.

3. Research the types of properties that are popular in the area: Determine what types of properties are in high demand in the area. For instance, *single-family homes* may be more popular in some areas, while *multi-unit buildings* may be in higher demand in others. Look for trends in property type and consider what type of property is likely to provide the best returns.

Challenges

1. Lack of knowledge about real estate markets in different locations: Investing in real estate in a new location can be challenging if you don't have a good understanding of the local market. Consider working with a *local real estate agent* who can provide insight into the market and help you make informed decisions.

2. Difficulty in identifying reliable sources of data for property values, rental rates, and housing demand: Finding accurate and reliable data on real estate markets can be challenging. Look for reputable sources of data, such as *online websites* or *real estate agents*, and be cautious of sources that may provide biased or incomplete information.

3. Understanding the nuances of different property types and their demand in different locations: Different types of properties may be in higher demand in different locations. For example, *multi-unit buildings* may be more popular in urban areas, while *single-family homes* may be more popular in suburban areas. It's important to understand these nuances to make informed investment decisions.

2. Set Budget

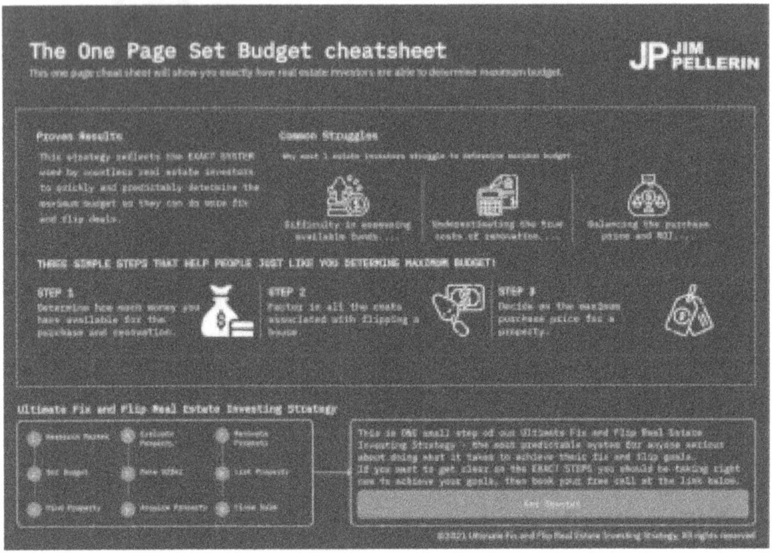

Flipping a property requires a significant amount of capital, so it's important to set a budget before you start looking for properties. This means determining how much money you have available for the purchase and renovation of a property. You should also factor in all the costs associated with flipping a house, including closing costs, renovation costs, and holding costs. Setting a realistic budget will help you narrow your search and find properties that are within your price range.

Steps

1. Determine how much money you have available for the purchase and renovation of a property: To determine your available funds, start by calculating your *total assets,* including cash, investments, and any lines of credit you may have available. Next, subtract any *outstanding* *debts* or liabilities to get a clear picture of your liquid assets. This will give you an idea of how much money you have available for a down payment and renovation costs.

2. Factor in ALL the costs associated with flipping a house: Flipping a property involves several costs, including the *purchase price* of the property, *closing costs*, *renovation costs*, and *holding costs*. Renovation costs can vary widely depending on the condition of the property and the extent of the renovations required. Holding costs include *property taxes*, *insurance*, *utilities*, and any *mortgage payments* or *interest on loans* used to finance the project. Be sure to factor in all of these costs when setting your budget.

3. Decide on a maximum purchase price for the property: Based on your available funds and the total costs associated with flipping a house, you can determine the maximum purchase price for the property. This will ensure that you can afford the property and still have enough money for renovations and holding costs. Keep in mind that the purchase price should also leave enough room for a potential profit when you sell the property.

Challenges

1. Difficulty in accurately assessing your available funds and assets: One solution could be to work with a *financial advisor* or *accountant* to help you calculate your available funds and assets accurately. You could also research and *compare financing options* to help you determine what type of loans or lines of credit you may qualify for.

2. Underestimating the true costs of renovation, closing costs, and holding costs: To avoid underestimating costs, it's important to research and gather *quotes from contractors* and service providers to get a realistic estimate of the renovation costs. It's also important to factor in all of the holding costs, including property taxes and insurance, when setting your budget.

3. Balancing the purchase price with the expected return on investment: This can be a challenge, as you don't want to overpay for a property and risk losing money on the project. To address this challenge, it's important to *research the real estate market* in the area and compare the purchase price of the property to similar properties in the area. You could also work with a *real estate agent* or *appraiser* to help you determine the potential value of the property after renovations.

3. Find Property

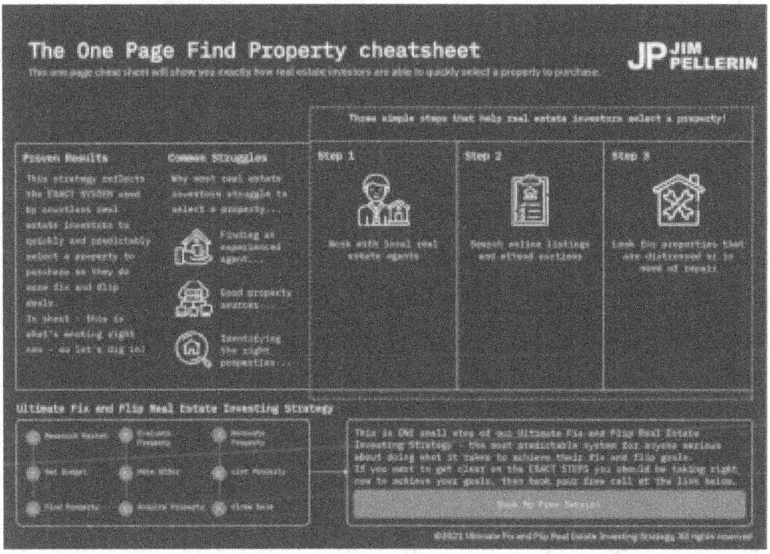

Once you have your budget set, it's time to start looking for a property to flip. There are many ways to find properties, including working with a real estate agent, searching online listings, and attending auctions. Look for properties that are distressed or in need of repair, as these are often the best candidates for flipping.

Steps

1. Work with a real estate agent: A real estate agent can help you find properties that meet your criteria and provide you with valuable insights about the *local real estate market*. Look for an agent who has experience working with fix-and-flip properties and can guide you through the process of purchasing a distressed property. They can also help you negotiate with the seller and ensure that the transaction goes smoothly.

2. Search online listings and attend auctions: Online listings and auctions are great sources of properties that are in need of repair. Many websites specialize in listing *distressed properties*, such as foreclosures or short sales. You can also attend auctions where foreclosed properties are sold to the highest bidder.

3. Look for properties that are distressed or in need of repair: Look for properties that are in need of repair or renovation, as these are often the best candidates for flipping. These properties may have been *foreclosed*, *abandoned*, or *neglected*, and they can be purchased at a discount. Keep in mind that the extent of repairs needed should be proportional to the potential increase in the property's value.

Challenges

1. Finding a real estate agent who has experience with fix-and-flip properties: It can be challenging to find a real estate agent who has experience working with fix-and-flip properties. Not all agents are familiar with the process, so it's important to do your research and find an agent who has a proven *track record* of working with investors who flip properties.

2. Finding accurate and up-to-date listings online: Online listings can sometimes be outdated or inaccurate, which can be frustrating when trying to find the right property. It's important to use reputable websites and verify the information before making any offers.

3. Identifying properties with the right balance of repair needs and potential for value increase: It can be difficult to find properties that have the right balance of repair needs and potential for value increase. Some properties may require more repairs than they are worth, while others may not have enough potential for a significant increase in value.

It's important to carefully evaluate each property and consider all the potential costs and returns before making a decision.

Acquisition

4. Evaluate Property

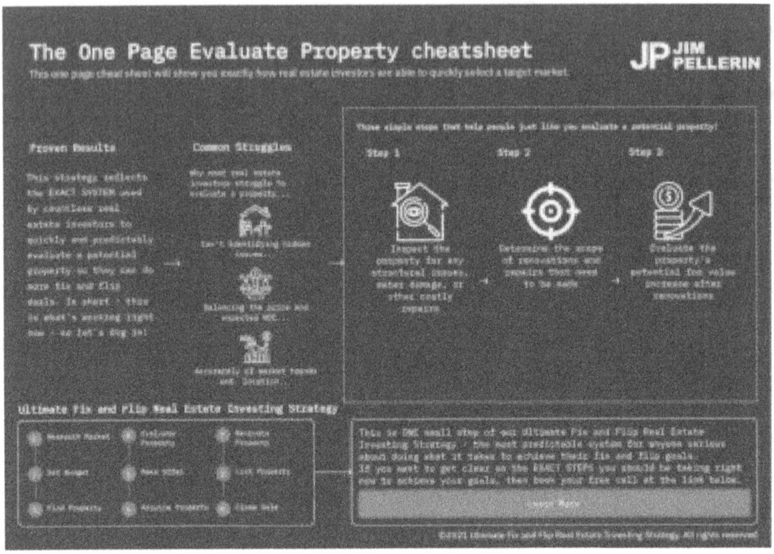

Before you make an offer on a property, it's important to thoroughly evaluate it. This means inspecting the property for any structural issues, water damage, or other costly repairs that may need to be made. You should also take note of any cosmetic changes that need to be made, such as updating the kitchen or bathrooms.

Steps

1. Inspect the property for any structural issues, water damage, or other costly repairs: This step involves hiring a professional *home inspector* or contractor to conduct a thorough examination of the property. The inspector will identify any structural issues, such as *foundation problems*, *roof leaks*, or *pest infestations*. They will also look for water damage, mold, and other signs of moisture problems, which can lead to costly repairs if left unchecked.

2. Determine the scope of cosmetic changes that need to be made: Once the property has been inspected for any structural or water damage issues, you should evaluate the cosmetic changes that need to be made. This includes *updating the kitchen*, *bathrooms*, *flooring*, and other areas of the property. You should also consider whether the property needs a fresh coat of *paint*, *new fixtures*, or *landscaping*.

3. Evaluate the property's potential for value increase after renovations: After identifying any repairs and cosmetic changes that need to be made, you should evaluate the potential for the property to increase in value after renovations. This involves researching the *local real estate market* to determine if the property is in a desirable location and if there is demand for renovated properties in the area.

Challenges

1. Identifying hidden issues that may not be apparent during an initial inspection: Sometimes, there may be hidden issues that are not visible during an initial inspection, such as plumbing or electrical problems. It's important to hire a *qualified inspector* who can identify these issues and provide an accurate estimate of the cost to repair them.

2. Balancing the need for cosmetic changes with the expected return on investment: It's important to strike a balance between making necessary cosmetic changes to the property and the expected return on investment. You don't want to *overspend on renovations* that won't add significant value to the property.

3. Accurately assessing the potential for value increase based on market trends and property location: The potential for value increase will depend on market trends and the property's location. It's important to research the *local real estate market* and consult with a *real estate agent* or *appraiser* to accurately assess the property's potential for value increase.

5. Make Offer

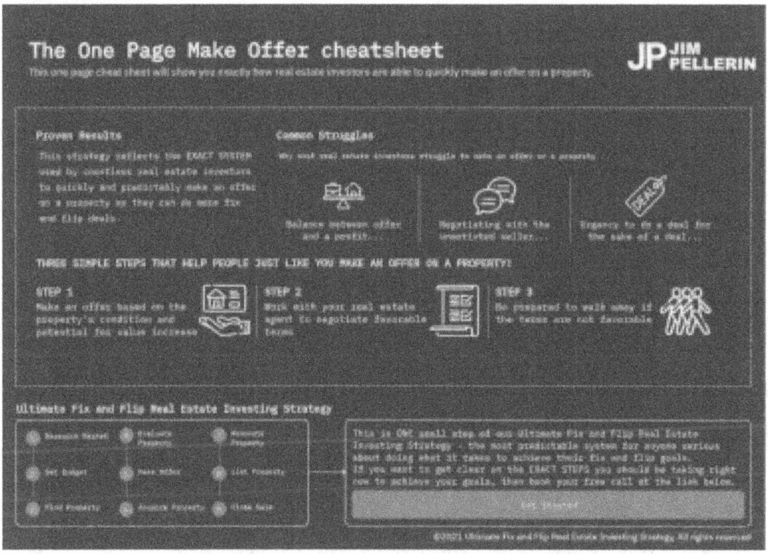

Once you've evaluated the property and determined that it's a good investment, it's time to make an offer. Be sure to take into account any repairs or renovations that need to be made when determining your offer price. You should also work with your real estate agent to negotiate favorable terms, such as a shorter closing period or a lower purchase price.

Steps

1. Determine your offer price based on the property's condition and potential for value increase: Your offer should be based on the current condition of the property and the estimated costs of repairs and renovations. You should also factor in the potential resale value after the renovations are complete. It's important to make an offer that is competitive but still allows for a profitable return on investment.

2. Work with your real estate agent to negotiate favorable terms: Your real estate agent can help you negotiate favorable terms, such as a shorter closing period or a lower purchase price. They can also help you navigate any counteroffers from the seller or their agent.

3. Be prepared to walk away if the terms are not favorable: If the seller is not willing to negotiate or the terms of the deal are not favorable, be prepared to walk away. It's important to protect your investment and not get caught up in a deal that is not profitable.

Challenges

1. Finding the right balance between a competitive offer and a profitable investment: Making an offer that is too low may not be accepted by the seller, while an offer that is too high can result in a lower return on investment. It's important to find the right balance between a competitive offer and a profitable investment.

2. Negotiating with the seller or their agent who may have different priorities: The seller or their agent may have different priorities than you, such as a *quick sale* or *a higher purchase price*. It's important to communicate your priorities and work with your real estate agent to negotiate favorable terms.

3. Balancing the desire to close the deal with the need to protect your investment: It's important to remember that flipping a house is a business investment, and not to get too emotionally invested in a deal. You should be *willing to walk away* if the terms of the deal are not favorable to protect your investment.

6. Acquire Property

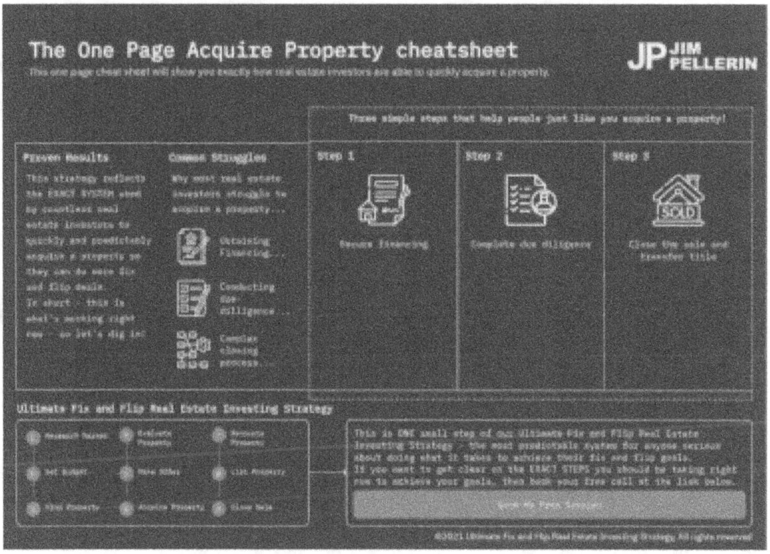

Once you've made an offer and the purchase and sale agreement is accepted, the next step is to secure financing and acquire the property. For financing, you should consider options such as a conventional mortgage, FHA loan, or hard money loan. You should also ensure that you have a solid understanding of the terms and conditions of the loan.

Once the financing is obtained and a property inspection is completed, the final step is to close the deal which includes the transfer of funds and the transfer of title.

Steps

1. **Secure financing:** After the purchase and sale agreement is accepted, you need to secure financing for the property. You can either pay for the property in cash or obtain a mortgage

from a lender. To obtain a mortgage, you will need to *provide financial information* and undergo a *credit check*. You may also need to provide a down payment for the property.

2. **Complete due diligence:** Before closing on the property, it's important to complete your due diligence. This may include a *property inspection*, *title search*, and *review of any existing leases* or rental agreements. This will help ensure that there are no hidden issues or liabilities with the property.
3. **Close the sale:** Once you have secured financing and completed your due diligence, you can proceed with closing the sale. This involves signing the necessary documents and paying any remaining fees or expenses associated with the purchase.

Challenges

1. **Difficulty obtaining Financing:** Obtaining financing can be a challenge, especially if you have a *limited credit history* or *low income*. You may need to shop around for lenders or consider alternative financing options such as private loans.
2. **Time for due diligence:** Completing due diligence can be time-consuming and expensive. It's important to be thorough, but this can also delay the acquisition process.
3. **Complex Closing Process:** Closing on a property can be a complex process involving multiple parties and legal documents. It's important to have a good understanding of the process and work with experienced professionals to ensure a smooth closing.

Profit

7. Renovate Property

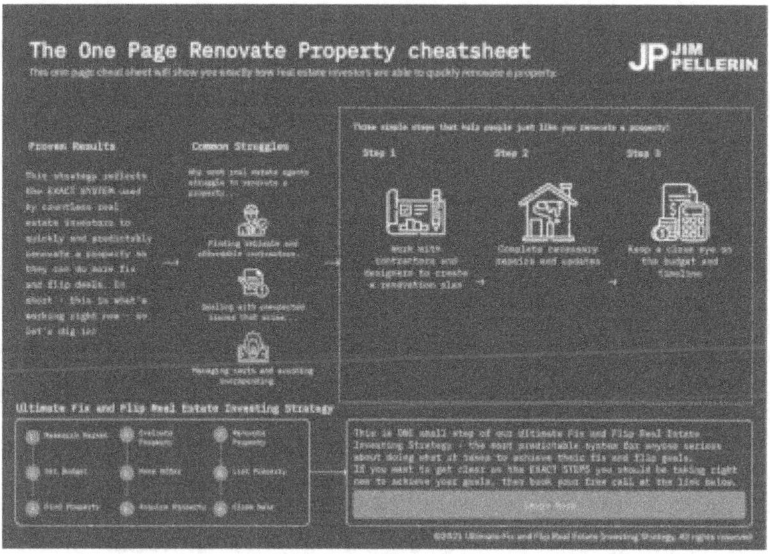

Once you've secured financing and closed on the property, it's time to start renovating. Work with contractors and designers to create a renovation plan that will increase the value of the property. This may include updating the kitchen and bathrooms, replacing flooring, and painting the interior and exterior of the property.

Steps

1. Work with contractors and designers to create a renovation plan: Meet with contractors and designers to discuss the scope of the renovation and create a plan that maximizes the value of the property within your budget.

2. Complete necessary repairs and updates: Ensure that all necessary repairs and updates are completed, including fixing *structural issues*, updating *electrical and plumbing systems*, replacing *damaged or outdated materials*, and *improving energy efficiency*.

3. Keep a close eye on the budget and timeline: Stay on top of the renovation budget and timeline by regularly *checking in with contractors*, *monitoring expenses*, and *adjusting the plan* as needed.

Challenges

1. Finding reliable and affordable contractors and designers: Finding contractors and designers who are reliable, affordable, and have experience working on flipping projects can be a challenge. It's important to do your research, *ask for references*, and carefully *vet potential contractors* before hiring them.

2. Dealing with unexpected issues that arise during renovation: It's common for unexpected issues to arise during the renovation process, such as discovering hidden damage or uncovering structural problems. This can cause delays and add to the cost of the project.

3. Managing costs and avoiding overspending on renovations: It's important to stick to the renovation budget and *avoid overspending on unnecessary upgrades* or materials. This requires careful planning and monitoring of expenses throughout the renovation process.

8. List Property

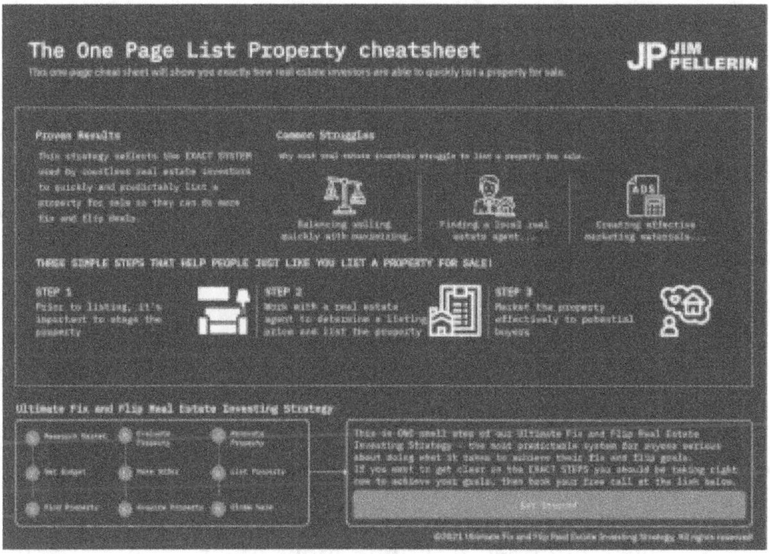

Once the renovations are complete, it's time to list it for sale. work with a real estate agent to market the property and find potential buyers. Your agent will help you set a competitive price for the property and create a marketing plan that will reach the right audience.

Steps

1. Prior to listing, it's important to stage the property: Staging involves decorating the property to make it more attractive to potential buyers. This may include adding *furniture*, *artwork*, and *accessories* to create a welcoming and inviting space. You may hire a professional stager to help with this process.

2. Work with a real estate agent to determine a listing price and list the property on multiple platforms: Your agent will help you set a competitive price for the property based on the current market conditions and the renovations you've made. They will also list the property on multiple platforms and other real estate websites to reach a wider audience.

3. Market the property effectively to potential buyers: Your agent will create effective marketing materials that highlight the property's features and potential. This may include *professional photos and videos*, *virtual tours*, *open houses*, and other marketing techniques to attract potential buyers.

Challenges

1. Balancing the desire to sell quickly with the need to maximize profit: It's important to find a balance between selling quickly and getting the best possible price for your property. Your real estate agent can help you make informed decisions about pricing and marketing strategies.

2. Finding a real estate agent who understands the local market and can effectively market the property: It's crucial to work with an experienced real estate agent who understands the local market and can help you navigate the selling process.

3. Creating effective marketing materials that highlight the property's features and potential: Creating effective marketing materials requires skill and experience. Your real estate agent should have a strong marketing plan in place to attract potential buyers and generate interest in your property.

9. Close Sale

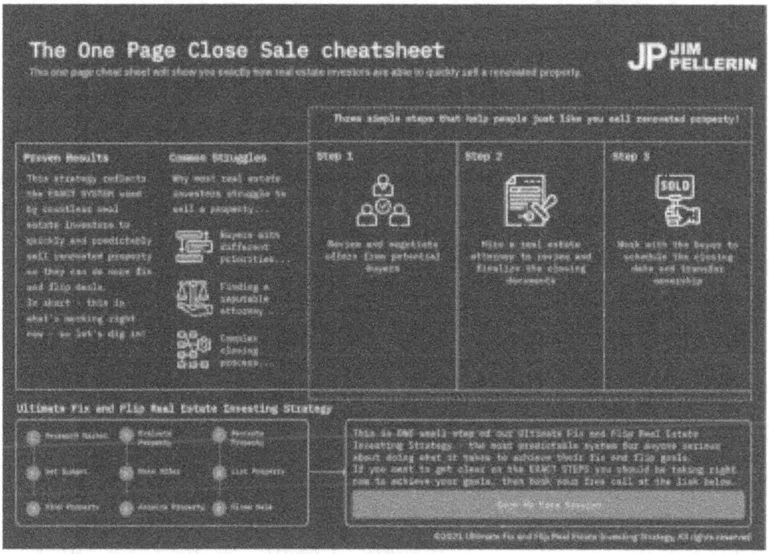

Once you've found a buyer, it's time to close the sale. This means finalizing all the paperwork and transferring ownership of the property to the new owner. Work with your real estate agent and lawyer to ensure a smooth and successful closing.

Steps

1. Review and negotiate offers from potential buyers: Once you receive offers from potential buyers, you should review them carefully and consider factors such as the *purchase price*, *terms* and *contingencies*. You may need to negotiate with the buyer to arrive at a mutually acceptable agreement.

2. Hire a real estate attorney to review and finalize the closing documents: A real estate attorney can review the *purchase agreement* and other *closing documents* to ensure that everything is in order and there are no legal issues that could cause problems later on.

3. Work with the buyer to schedule the closing date and transfer ownership: The closing date is the date when ownership of the property is officially transferred to the buyer. You will need to work with the buyer, their agent, and your attorney to ensure that all the *necessary paperwork is completed*, *funds are transferred*, and the property is *officially transferred* to the new owner.

Challenges

1. Negotiating with potential buyers who may have different priorities: Buyers may have different priorities when it comes to the purchase of a property, such as the *purchase price*, *closing date*, and *contingencies*. Negotiating with buyers to arrive at a mutually acceptable agreement can be a challenge, especially if there are multiple offers on the table.

2. Finding a reputable and experienced real estate attorney to review the closing documents: Hiring the right attorney is crucial to ensuring a smooth and successful closing. However, finding a reputable and experienced attorney can be challenging, especially if you are unfamiliar with flipping real estate.

3. Managing the logistics of the closing process, including scheduling and coordinating with the buyer: Closing a sale can be a complex and time-consuming process that involves *coordinating with multiple parties*, including the buyer, their agent, your attorney, and any lenders involved. Managing the logistics of the closing process can be a challenge, especially if there are unexpected issues that arise.

About The Author

JIM PELLERIN started real estate investing over twenty years ago. Since then, he has bought and sold millions of dollars of real estate. He began by purchasing and renting out duplexes. Following that he added Lease Options to his strategy. He has implemented many creative funding strategies that have allowed him to continue implementing various strategies and alloqed him to build a sizable portfolio.

As part of his education, he has attended numerous seminars on real estate investing, project management, property management, financing, renovations, motivation, time management, and many more. He has also read over 500 books on similar topics.

This book blends his experience and the knowledge he has gained through his investments and studies.

Visit his author page to discover my other publications: books2read.com/JimPellerin[1]

1. https://books2read.com/JimPellerin

Other Books By Jim Pellerin

Real Estate Investing: Strategies – The Secret to Financial Independence with Real Estate

books2read.com/strategies[1]

1. https://books2read.com/strategies

Real Estate Investing with Lease Options – How to Invest with No Money Down

books2read.com/Lease-Options[2]

2. https://books2read.com/Lease-Options

Invest NOW – The Passive Approach to Winning with Real Estate

books2read.com/investnow[3]

3. https://books2read.com/investnow

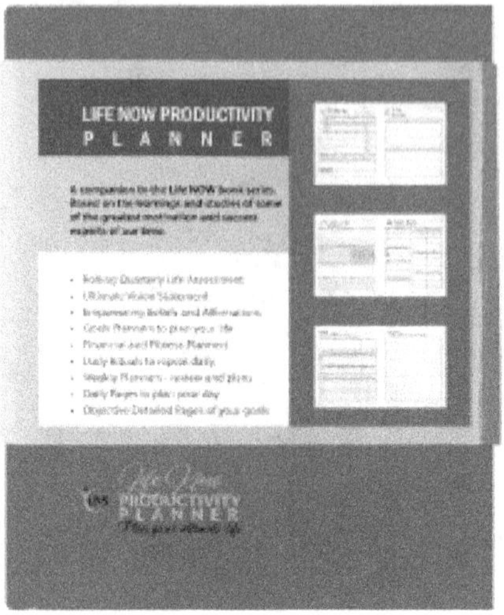

books2read.com/JimPellerin[4]

4. https://books2read.com/JimPellerin

Don't miss out!

Visit the website below and you can sign up to receive emails whenever Jim Pellerin publishes a new book. There's no charge and no obligation.

https://books2read.com/r/B-A-WGIX-ESWIC

BOOKS 2 READ

Connecting independent readers to independent writers.

Did you love *The Ultimate Beginners Guide to Fix and Flip Real Estate Investing*? Then you should read *Real Estate Investing Strategies: The Secret to Financial Independence with Real Estate*[5] by Jim Pellerin!

[6]

The mechanics of Real Estate Investing is simple: Buy a house and do something with it. Fix it and rent it, or just sell it. Sounds simple, doesn't it? Yet only a small percentage of us have enough courage to go out and take advantage of the opportunities that are available to us. Real Estate Investing can be more promising than stocks, bonds, and various other securities because of the higher rates of return.

In this book, I show you how to get started by describing the different types of skills you need, by showing you how to take control of your personal and financial situation, and by helping you decide what type of real estate investing you want to get involved in. I also show

---

5. https://books2read.com/u/m2QyNG

6. https://books2read.com/u/m2QyNG

you how to find properties, how to analyze them, and how to make an offer that makes sense. And finally, I describe what you need to do to manage your investment and ultimately how to sell your investment for the most profit.

I have been involved in real estate investing for over 20 years. I have yet to find a book that focuses on the investor and the overall process. Sure, there are lots of books on fix and flips, buy, rent and hold, rent to own, etc. However, I haven't found any good books on how to really get started in the real estate investing process from a practical viewpoint. The technical aspects of real estate investing are really quite easy. But if it's so easy, then why isn't everyone doing it?

This book is for people who are serious about getting started in real estate investing and who want to join the 5% of those who actually take action and invest. This book provides a strategic approach with the tried and tested methods and principles that have helped others make millions in real estate.

Read more at www.jimpellerin.com.

Also by Jim Pellerin

Real Estate Investing

Real Estate Investing Strategies: The Secret to Financial Independence with Real Estate

Real Estate Investing with Lease Options - Investing in Real Estate with No Money Down

Invest Now - The Passive Approach to Winning at Real Estate

The Ultimate Beginners Guide to Real Estate Investing

The 98 Best Real Estate Investing Strategies

The Ultimate Beginners Guide to Wholesale Real Estate Investing

The Ultimate Beginners Guide to Rental Real Estate Investing

The Ultimate Beginners Guide to Fix and Flip Real Estate Investing

Watch for more at www.jimpellerin.com.

www.ingramcontent.com/pod-product-compliance
Lightning Source LLC
LaVergne TN
LVHW022041200926
848481LV00003B/734
9798223705499